Creativity
in the
Music Classroom

Creativity in the Music Classroom

The Best of MEJ

Donald L. Hamann, Editor

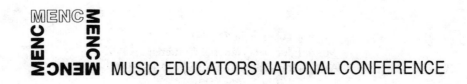 MUSIC EDUCATORS NATIONAL CONFERENCE

Book design by Karen M. Fields

Contents

Introduction

by Donald L. Hamann

I n his book *The Closing of the American Mind,* Allan Bloom states that "What defines man is no longer his reason...but his art, for in art man can be said to be creative. There he brings order to chaos. The greatest men are not the knowers but the artists...."[1] As individuals in a world of change, we all have a need to bring, through the arts, order to chaos and to define greatness by the creative artistic endeavors of individualistic effort. The desire to foster individual creativity, to develop creative skills, and to be immersed in creative thought is not unique to any time or age. We are a nation, like nations before us, that has treasured the gift of creativity without necessarily understanding it or providing for it. It is for these reasons that we focus on the topic of creativity in this collection—to help us better understand the gift of creativity and to help us focus, stimulate discussion, and provide a forum in which further creative thought may develop. In order to better understand the role that creativity plays in our society and in our educational system, we need to look at the arts, for it is through the study of the arts that creativity is allowed a forum in which to prosper and develop.

The MENC petition "Music Makes the Difference: A Declaration of Concern About Music Education," which was presented to Congress and the administration in March 1991, contains the statement "music and the other arts have been recognized as unique to human capabilities and creativity...."[2] It is a commonly held belief that there is a relationship between creativity and study in the arts. Some of the most treasured creative possessions are those from the fields of music, art, drama, theater, and dance.

While other disciplines have banned individuals known for their creative thoughts, it is the arts to which people turn for their creative inspiration. The arts not only allow but demand that a certain level of individualism—creativity—be evident in works deemed to be of lasting value. The concept of creativity in the arts is not merely a construct to be addressed in the confines of the material presentation; it is, rather, a modus operandi. In music, art, drama, and theater classrooms across the country, teachers attempt to direct, instill, develop, and inspire creativity in all individuals. From the seeds sown in these classrooms grow the future artists and the creative work force of a nation. The importance of providing articles that can help teachers guide individuals in the development of their creative potentials is clear. For this reason, a significant portion of this collection is devoted to "how to" articles, and five such articles are found in the last section of the book.

It would be difficult to find arts educators or administrators who do not believe that participation in arts can enhance individuals' creative abilities, but even though the study of creativity in the arts seems to be central to the discipline, research in this area has been limited. Few research studies have been designed to determine the relationship between the study of arts and creativity. In general, researchers have found the following relationships to exist between creativity and study in specific discipline areas such as music, drama, art, and theater:[3]

- The more arts experience an individual has, in general, the higher his or her creativity score tends to be.

• The more music experience an individual has, the higher his or her creativity score tends to be.

• The study and use of improvisational techniques tend to be positively related to higher creativity scores.

• Creativity scores are positively related to measures of general intelligence and achievement.

Creative thinking and the ability to creatively discover and produce remains one of the most important components of human development and survival. The articles selected for this collection, spanning a quarter-century of thought on the topic of creativity, are divided into the following sections:

1. Philosophical Support for Creativity in the Music Classroom

2. Definition: Creativity—What Is It?

3. Creativity and the Curriculum

4. Incorporating Creativity in the Classroom

The importance of this collection of some of the best articles on creativity published in the *Music Educators Journal* is twofold. First, I hope that this collection of articles will serve as a reference to those interested in refreshing or further expanding their knowledge of creativity in the field of music. Second, I believe that through the review and reading of these articles, further creative thoughts and ideas will be generated and shared with thousands of individual students in many classrooms. It is said that fine wine, nurtured and cared for in the proper environment, will blossom and develop gracefully with age. The proper development of individual creativity also requires an environment of nurturing and caring. It is hoped that this collection of articles will generate stimulating thought and discussion from

which the seeds of creativity will blossom. In a nurturing and caring environment, the fruits of individual creativity will develop and age gracefully through a lifetime.

Notes

1. Allan Bloom, *The Closing of the American Mind* (New York: Simon and Schuster, 1987), 180–81.

2. "Music Makes the Difference," *MENC Soundpost* 7, no. 1 (Fall 1990): 3.

3. Although there are authors who have devised measures of musical creativity or have attempted to determine whether one approach was more conducive to enhancing creativity than another, few authors have attempted to determine whether a relationship exists between study in the arts and measures of creativity. The following articles are suggested reading in this area: S. M. Gibson, "A Comparison of Music and Multiple Arts Experiences in the Development of Creativity in Middle School Students" (Doctoral diss., Washington University, 1989); Donald L. Hamann, Richard Bourassa, and Mark Aderman, "Creativity and the Arts," *Dialogue in Instrumental Music Education* 14, no. 2, (1990): 59–68; Donald L. Hamann, Richard Bourassa, and Mark Aderman, "The Relationship of 'Arts' Experiences and Creativity Scores of High School Students," *Contributions in Music Education* (in press); Cynthia D. Howell, "The Relationship Between Arts Education and Creativity Among High School Students" (Ed.D. diss., University of Northern Colorado, 1990); Carol P. Richardson, "Creativity Research in Music Education: A Review," *Bulletin of the Council for Research in Music Education*, no. 74, (Spring 1983): 1–21; James Roderick, "An Investigation of Selected Factors of the Creative Thinking Ability of Majors in a Teacher Training Program" (Ed.D. diss., University of Illinois at Urbana-Champaign, 1965); M. L. Silverman, "Ensemble Improvisation as a Creative Technique in the Secondary Instrumental Music Program" (Ed.D. diss., Stanford University, 1962); Donald J. Simpson, "The Effect of Selected Musi-

cal Studies on Growth in General Creative Potential" (Ed.D. diss., University of Southern California, 1969); Edward A. Tarratus, Jr., "Creative Processes in Music and the Identification of Creative Music Students" (Ph.D. diss, Ohio State University, 1964); Karen L. Wolff, "The Effects of General Music Education on the Academic Achievement, Perceptual-Motor Development, Creative Thinking, and School Attendance of First-Grade Children" (Ph.D. diss., University of Michigan, 1979).

Donald L. Hamann is associate professor of music education at Kent State University, Kent, Ohio.

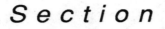

Section

Philosophical Support for Creativity in the Music Classroom

This first section begins with a philosophical overview of the concept of creativity. The three articles chosen for this overview are thought-provoking and help frame the content of the book from a philosophical point of view.

In this excellent article, Robert W. Sherman provides us with a philosophy of creativity and a definition of what creativity is as he helps us understand its nature. In the course of his discussion, Sherman points out several important concepts and elaborates on them:

- Creativity can't be taught, but in the proper environment and with the proper guidance and support, it can flourish and grow.

- Knowing about creative individuals and the creative process too often is more important in the music curriculum than is the actual process of creativity. As a result, the creative process in music frequently occurs only outside the music building and the "established" music curriculum.

- For creative activity to be effective, it must be an integral part of the curriculum and not an added component. The idea that students must be molded into certain patterns as apprentices shatters the framework of creativity—creativity is not the product of a student who apprentices under a formidable taskmaster.

- Creative individuals are often feared because they are different.

Creativity and the Condition of Knowing in Music

Robert W. Sherman

The transformation of a talented but callow young person into a knowing musician is profoundly mysterious, and being so, gives cause for much misunderstanding. Basic to the confusion are conflicting ideas concerning the primary goal of education in music. It is a generally accepted notion that the purpose of music education is the formation of a knowledgeable musician. This is not an entirely unworthy goal; however, it is only half of the total equation that begins with knowing. The problem begins when the state of being knowledgeable is confused with the state of knowing. Although typical dictionary definitions of the two terms imply interchangeable usage, knowing and being knowledgeable are used here to describe differing conditions of the intellect. A knowing musician is understood to be one who knows music; a knowledgeable musician is one who knows about music. The two conditions are most clearly separated in the musician by the manner in which they find expression. Knowing is expressed in music through composing and performing; it is a quality of understanding that is communicable but cannot be verbalized. Being knowledgeable is expressed through verbalization. It is the kind of understanding that may be illuminated by knowing but is entirely nonmusical.

The Condition of Knowing

Knowing is a cultivated condition; it is nourished by the kind of doing that begets discovery, tempered by the kind of success and failure that strengthens character, subject to the kind of aloneness that encourages

Robert W. Sherman is the former head of the Department of Music Theory and Composition, Ball State University, Muncie, Indiana. He is now retired and lives in Spring Hill, Florida. This article originally appeared in the October 1971 Music Educators Journal.

contemplation. It is the result of all that may be associated with creative activity. In a sense, knowing is the result of one's coming to grips personally with things and ideas in ways that reflect individualized assessments and decisions. Within the context of our educational institutions, we cannot teach creativity, or otherwise transfer knowing from one individual to another, but we can encourage it by establishing the conditions under which it may exist, and we can stimulate it and to some degree guide it. Assisted or unassisted, the path to knowing is made by and traveled alone by the person who seeks to know. Only when a degree of knowing is achieved can the individual begin to make wise and profitable use of the experience of others.

The refinements that have taken place over the centuries in the process of producing the educated person have been directed almost entirely at developing convenient ways to discourage the student from finding out things for herself or himself. For too long the main thrust of education has been concerned with the transferal of knowledge. The inference to be made from this particular preoccupation with knowledge is that there is no longer a need for a person to go where people have been, to do what people have done, or to experience what people have experienced. It is assumed, for example, that a person no longer must have the experience of living in the jungle to know the jungle—that knowledge about the jungle is sufficient. Victims of this quest for knowledge entirely at the expense of knowing become classic examples of the educated fool. Fortunately, there will always be some individuals in whom the creative instinct is strong and to whom inventiveness is a way of life. These people remain immune to the restrictions and prescriptions of much formal education; the less strong do not.

Creative Involvement in Music

The story of education in music, despite all the claimed uniqueness, is no different from the story of education in any area of learning. Most, if not all, genuinely creative activity—that which leads to knowing in music—takes place outside the aegis of institutionalized learning. To some, this activity is looked upon as illicit behavior and a threat to the institution. The most obvious example of this is the secondary school student who prefers to know music on the level of rock through creative involvement outside school rather than to know *about* music on whatever level it is presented in school. One might opine that had music and music education developed along more creative lines, students would look to the schools as the prime source of musical excitement and imagination.

Though one may function creatively in any area of music, most musicians have limited their concept of creative activity to the act of composing. Within the educational system, composing is generally done by only the professed student composers, but even then, not until they have "learned enough about music to do it." This is a most regrettable practice; that it has survived so long is incredible. Happily, during the decade of the 1960s, the creative muse gave birth to little pockets of activity within the educational establishment of this country. The great majority of these are totally honest attempts to breathe life into a tired, old system. Much of what is done, though it has the outward appearance of creativity, functions more as imitative gestures within the framework of what might be called applied statistics. This is a kind of activity that is related to the idea of painting by the numbers.

A Spirit of Change

However short of the mark some efforts toward genuine creativity may fall, the spirit of creativity is at work nevertheless. Music education, along with the entire world of music, has been so attached to the "great monuments" concept that it is to be expected that initial attempts to bring creative activity into the classroom should still be rooted in the same ideal. Genuinely creative activity is difficult to accept within the educational establishment because it is basically the kind of activity that is anti-establishment by nature. However, it is also the most traditional kind of activity within the arts. The educational establishment by nature is static; the characteristic necessities of structuring common to most types of institutions today tend to freeze a subject area. Creative activity, by fostering the tradition of change, becomes a source of irritation.

In spite of the gestures being made toward creativity in music education and the increasing numbers of creative individuals who have become part of the educational establishment, the creative student and teacher generally exist in a hostile environment. The behavioral patterns and thought processes of the creative, being different, give rise to rumors and suspicions; to some they become a threat. Human nature being what it is, we must expect the fear and insecurity of the noncreative to continue, regardless of what changes occur in the field of education. Still, we can and must remove whatever obstacles stand as deterrents to the eventual inclusion of creative activity as an integral part of all music education.

For creative activity to be effective in music education, it cannot simply be added to what presently exists in the educational process and be made to function as a competitive avenue of learning. It is imperative that the education of the musician and listener alike be thought out anew. The creative and critical faculties of the student must be cultivated by learning situations that allow the one faculty to complement the other. The structuring of an effective course of study and the development of the teaching techniques used within it is in itself an example of the creative act refined by good judgment. Such a course of study must allow each individual, insofar as his or her talents and mentality will permit, to know music and subsequently profit from knowing about music. Such a course must be of one piece, of whole cloth, fashioned to lead people to the creation and comprehension of the noblest expression they can attain by means of music; it cannot be a patchwork quilt designed to protect them from the effects of their own times. Such a course must relate to people and to the arts as they are now, not as they might have been yesterday.

Originality, Not Mimicry

Creativity as a means to learning is certainly not new to education; its general nature and function, however, remain persistently misunderstood. Creativity, when related to the teaching process, is customarily intended to provide a means of achieving a desired end with the least amount of fuss and time. The desired end is efficiency, a goal that taxes the creative imagination of the teacher in prethinking and preorganizing and reduces the possibility of creative effort and discovery on the part of the student. When the idea of creativity is associated with the student, it is generally misconstrued to mean mimicry. It is quite obvious that both of these concepts of creative activity, though well-intentioned, encourage mental servitude. Why should such ventures into the creative realm serve only to produce undesirable results? More important, why are so many students and teachers deluded into believing that the creative faculty has been genuinely exercised when they participate in these ventures?

Music does not grow on trees, is not harvested in the fields, nor is it extracted from the ground: music is not a product of nature and does not exist outside of the mind. Music came to be and remains a product of people's imaginations. Music is sound made fanciful by the manipulations of the individual human mind; it is an art form in which conception on the part of the composer, performer, and listener is based on the esthesia of the individual—his or her capacity for feeling. Such a premise makes vital the notion that anyone in the music profession, whether composer, performer, teacher, or student, must function within a framework of mutual respect for an individual's point of view concerning what music is and how one treats it. Point of view does not mean the quick and idle opinionating practiced by some, but rather quality of understanding (the knowing) that develops from genuine creative involvement.

Efficiency and mimicry fail to cultivate the knowing musician—one who creates and performs with imagination and critical judgment—because, as concepts, they are the result of misapplications of simplicity and authenticity. They fail also because, by both, students are conditioned to rely on an authority outside themselves. The students are not regarded as contributing members of the operation, or even as individuals who react. The only way the students can comprehend music is through their own senses and intellects. The vantage points from which they create, perform, or listen are their own; they are each very much alone no matter how close they may seem to be to others. Each person's point of view must be a factor; it must be respected. Unless music is to be taught into a state of oblivion, educators must realize that one of the prime functions of teaching music is to assist each student in the development of a point of view, rather than to force one on him or her for adoption.

The Place of Music in the Curriculm

Improperly used authority does not take into account the premise that knowing illuminates knowledge. Students should learn to select and manipulate the materials of music through composing and performing before concerning themselves with how others have done it. Students also should have a knowing awareness of a principle before they are confronted with information about the manner in which others have applied it. One of the prime reasons some seemingly talented students never understand music or develop any degree of musical resourcefulness is that they have been placed under the yoke of a dominating teacher who envisions himself or herself as a crusading taste maker. Such a teacher insists on having students compose, perform, or even listen according to the manner of the teacher or others in authority. Such students are never allowed to work out solutions of their own; they become forever dependent on others. By contrast, the teacher who stimulates the student's imagination through creative problem-solving is the teacher who prepares the student for a life of continued growth and accomplishment.

One of the most controversial aspects of music teaching—one that becomes an issue at all levels of instruction—concerns the place of contemporary music in the music curriculum. At the moment, music education is historically oriented and, consequently, places contemporary music at the end of the line. Except for a handful of secondary schools and universities, contemporary music, when it is encountered, is dealt with rather superficially and most often as a curiosity in the otherwise sane world of music. Educators would rather preserve the image of past cultures through their students than assist them in developing the

means of making, performing, and comprehending the music of their own culture.

People's natural desire to preserve the musical art becomes a misguided mania when youth resists change and the adult longs for a return to the "good old days." Such conservatism implies a belief that each individual, consciously or otherwise, assumes he or she was born into a fully developed and totally stabilized artistic culture. History shows that the only tradition having any semblance of constancy is the tradition of change. All the values of art are relative, and the artistic culture of any people at any time is in a state of evolution. Music is a living, vital, ever-changing, many-faceted conceptual medium of expression. Whatever the intrinsic value of a musical work of a past age, it remains an expression of the age in which it was conceived. What we understand and appreciate about older music is affected by what we know today; there is, in a sense, no way to create authenticity in either the presentation or reception of it.

> *Most, if not all, genuinely creative activity . . . takes place outside the aegis of institutionalized learning.*

Appreciating the Present

It is certainly natural to maintain an interest in the accomplishments of antecedent cultures; it is most unnatural, however, for generations of people to be encouraged by an educational system that abrogates the artworks of their own culture in order to sustain those of the past. The circumstances that have caused the long siege of uncreative dependence on the past are both complex and unimportant. What emerges from all this as simple and extremely important is that music education must abandon its obsession with the past and address itself to the problems and needs of the young of today's world. Music education must assist in the task of restoring students' faith in today, their hope in tomorrow, and their respect for yesterday. The key to it all is the present; it unlocks the doors to what was and what will be in music.

In this second article of a three-part series, Robert W. Sherman discusses the importance of including creativity in a properly balanced music curriculum. Believing that the purpose of including an active creative component in a music curriculum is not only to find the creative artists of the future but also to help enhance the creative efforts of all students, Sherman states, "Rather than regard music as a process that is as natural and vital to all people as verbal expression, we have made its basic function an optional addendum to our behavior patterns." One problem he has identified in many music curriculums is that the creative musical act is too often used to foster selective development of individuals for the concert hall, who in turn perform for a select few.

Creativity and the Condition of Knowing in Music

PART 2

by Robert W. Sherman

The compulsive drive to effect change seems to have captivated every segment of our society and is being directed at every kind of endeavor. Education in general and music education in particular are well within the stream of this activity. Reform in music education is badly needed, and even the most insensitive among us are aware of something amiss in the world of music.

Fostering the Musical Art

The desire to bring music to the child in school, a most worthy goal, has fostered certain practices that are coming to be recognized as the most basic or underlying causes of problems in music education. No matter what the level of instruction, much of the educational philosophy that has emerged over the years as a result of collective teaching practices

Robert W. Sherman is the former head of the Department of Music Theory and Composition, Ball State University, Muncie, Indiana. He is now retired and lives in Spring Hill, Florida. This article originally appeared in the November 1971 Music Educators Journal.

presents music as something already made—the product of many older and generally foreign cultures and a thing apart from the student. Music is treated as though it were a ready-to-wear garment that will change the character and intellectual demeanor of the wearer. This has resulted in the serious disparity that exists between the cultural derivation of the musical art as we attempt to practice it and our culture as it exists. Whatever rationale one may use to claim a healthy state of the musical arts, there is little evidence exhibited in the ordinary course of public events that a viable music culture even exists except in terms of popular music, which uses, as two of its keys to success, market analysis and large-scale promotion. What exists as music in the public concert halls is becoming more and more unrelated to what exists as music in the schools; the two of these are totally unrelated to what exists as music in public communication. Educators at all levels must eliminate the kind of irrelevance to society that is fostered by adhering to antiquated and ineffectual programs of instruction and to static approaches to curricular development; those involved in the activities of our concert halls must eliminate the tendency toward snobbish alliances with the past and fearful avoidance of the creative works of our own time; and those in the field of public communication must cease confusing the need for relevance with the obvious pursuit of crass commercialism. The estrangement in this potent trio must give way to a cooperative effort to solve a problem that is more serious than any will admit. Simply stated, the problem is this: How do we foster the development of a musical art of high and demanding quality that emanates from our own culture and commands the respect and support of the people?

Music as a Creative Process

The attempts of educators to stimulate an interest in music by focusing on the entertainment aspect of popular music, or to appeal to the sociological urge for personal involvement through ethnically oriented musical studies and pseudo-folk music, though well intended, do little more than put off the search for more reasonable and effective solutions. By emphasizing these and other sociologically oriented diversions, we obscure one of the most fundamental and pressing needs of our time—a return to the full consideration of music as a creative art and the realization that the creative process itself is not only a truly high-gain manner of learning but the surest means of getting to know music.

A properly balanced music curriculum should require creativity—not for the purpose of ferreting out the creative artists of the future, but for what the act of making can do for the student. In the guise of maintaining standards of quality in the musical arts, we have "protected" music from the corruptive toying of schoolchildren. Rather than regard music as a process that is as natural and vital to all people as verbal expression, we have made its basic function an optional addendum to our behavior patterns. We have thus become a nation of passive spectators to an art that has degenerated to the level of commonplace, banal entertainment. To assuage our consciences in this, we have raised such entertainment to a place of eminence in our lives.

The Necessity of Change

Although change may take place at any point in the total music curriculum, the most effective ways to

initiate the changes that will bring about the needed balance are, first, through the college and university teacher education programs, and second, through in-service programs. Paradoxically, these call for beginning at points in the educational cycle where the change to a creative approach to music education will meet with the most resistance. Nevertheless, if the changes that are needed throughout the elementary and secondary schools are to be brought about, we must prepare teachers who are sympathetic to the needed changes and capable of effecting them.

A great deal of the fault in music teacher preparation is not so much a matter of balance in the amount of theory, performance, literature, and methods as it is a matter of how these study areas are taught and what purposes they are to serve. With the advent of musicology there began a grand treasure hunt that has rendered extant a great quantity of the music written since the beginning of recorded history. We now find that most of the university faculties in all four study areas are comfortably settled in a routine dedication to the care and preservation of old music. At this point in time, the universities cannot be so preoccupied with the past and expect to succeed in the task of preparing teachers for the future. The teachers of music in our universities, whatever their particular specialties or interests, must come to realize that they exist for the purpose of bringing students into a relationship with music that will promote an enthusiastic and lasting drive to perpetuate music as a living and totally practiced art. The art is perpetuated in the theory classroom by the creative involvement of the student in the act of composition, in the study of performance by the constant evolution of instrumental technique and the performance of new music, in the study of literature by making known and supporting new music, and in the methods classes by the development of teaching techniques that will emphasize the creative involvement of students at all grade levels.

Exercising the Imagination

Music theory for the freshman and sophomore must be primarily a course in creative problem-solving (the free exercise of the student's imagination in the manipulation of given materials and principles as they exist). Music theory taught in this way requires a redefinition of goals, a new concept of what constitutes materials and principles in music, and a complete reassessment of the student-teacher relationship. The latter is perhaps the most difficult to achieve. First of all, the young men and women entering the university are unique personalities, each a curious mixture of talent, intellect, desire, dedication, and resourcefulness; each variously garnished with a layer of prejudice; each oriented to a particular musical subculture; each generously endowed with a number of popular misconceptions about music; and each subject to his or her own brand of fear. Second, in spite of the popularization of the "rebelliousness" of students by the news media and the customary lack of esteem with which students have regarded music theory over the years, a substantial number of students, by nature or conditioning, are very pro-status quo. The noncreative, style-oriented approach to lower division theory instruction, by the very nature of its being part of the scene as each generation of students enters it, has been tolerated and accepted as a necessary rigor of the academic environment in music. Music theory, so little changed during the twentieth century, has been surrounded by an aura that suggests divine intervention. Seemingly, being so regarded, it is held in the protective custody of the university and used as part of a survival rite for those on the way to musical maturity.

Even though the noncreative, stylistic approach to music theory instruction is pointless busywork to the creatively imaginative student and instructor alike, there is a definite stigma attached to the idea of change. The less imaginative student and instructor, to whom the old practices have held out a hope for eventual musical understanding and to whom "knowing about" becomes an acceptable substitute for "knowing," may react fearfully to change. Consequently, it is not enough for the instructor to adopt the philosophy of a "create and discover" approach to music theory; he or she must, aside from having the expected expertise, cultivate the patience and understanding that will make it work.

The Instructor's Role

The proper role of an instructor is to provide the circumstances by which students can learn to think and to compose music generated by their own peculiar and discovered conceptualizations of the creative process. There is really nothing within the art of music that individuals cannot learn about by themselves. Left to their own devices, interested individuals would acquire knowledge of music to the degree that their particular life patterns would provide the needs and circumstances for learning. Learning left entirely to the nature of local needs and conditions would provide limited experience and allow equally limited achievement for all. By institutionalizing education we do not change the nature of learning; we change only the conditions under which it may take place. An institution's success is measured, therefore, by the degree to which it facilitates natural discovery by the student.

Whereas people were once privileged to drink from the cup of knowledge, they are now compelled to swim in an ocean of it. Whether they remain afloat depends on whether education progresses from an information-gathering and memorizing system to a functional, process-oriented system. Such a progression is necessary to avert the further spread of intellectual and psychological isolationism in young people—the kind of isolationism or cop-out that is evidenced by the numerous behaviors, from passive rejection to harmfully antisocial actions, used to escape the realities of the world. This climate of escapism suggests that the intellectual and psychological preparedness of the student to meet and cope with the manifold realities of the world of music must be the primary goal of college courses in music theory. A student so prepared has developed a functional grasp of the principles that are basic to the contemporary form of the art, is accustomed to problem solving, and is willing to venture into the unfamiliar.

What Are the Fundamentals?

To achieve this goal, music educators must develop a new concept of what constitutes the content or material of a theory course and a new understanding of what principals are fundamental to the art. A first step is to consider the undesirability of regarding information as the content of a theory course. The gathering of information for its own sake, once a respected social and intellectual grace, is now an occupation of value to none but the musical dilettante. Information, however it comes into being, is topical by nature, and during the period of its usefulness, is subject to all the conflicting and evolving concepts of those who deal with it. When something is regarded as a "fact" or "precept" in music, this something is nothing more than the best information or best solution available at a given time. Change is inevitable, and today's factual data or operating premise may well become an item of misinformation or an inappropriate precept tomorrow. An information-oriented course, therefore, is merely an attempt to establish a brain bank of stock solutions to old problems that hopefully will serve as a contingency fund for use against the time when the same problems may arise again. Unfortunately, circumstances are seldom such that a problem will yield to a memorized solution, and unused information is soon cast into oblivion. The transient quality of knowledge per se is graphically expressed by Alfred North Whitehead in *The Aims of Education* when he describes it as something that "keeps no better than fish."

The vocabulary used in the music studio or classroom indicates that much of what is presently regarded as the "basic materials" or the "fundamentals" of music is neither basic as material nor fundamental to music. Whatever importance one might attach to such items as intervals, scales, chords, and key signatures, they are special-case materials that are peculiar to music of various types but not fundamental to any of them. Therefore, the classification of such music-related phenomena as basic material or fundamental, besides representing shoddy scholarship, establishes a most subtle though unintentional bias in the student's concept of music. Though some musicians possess an instinctive awareness that renders them immune to things inaccurate and irrelevant, the misconceptions cultivated by this bias serve as formidable obstacles to the creative activity and potential development of many. Since the vast majority of students are introduced to music at a level considerably above what is truly basic, they are channeled into a system in which much of what should individualize their musical aesthetics is already decided for them. Few students ever have the opportunity to contemplate and work with the simple, basic materials of music—sound and silence.

Active Involvement with Process

Sound and silence must be thought of as abstractions—as the idea of sound and the idea of silence. This conceptualization emphasizes the fact that *any* sound, whether a simple sine wave or a complex sonority, is potentially usable as music material. Silence becomes music material when it is enclosed by sound, a concept similar to negative space in sculpture. It is implicit, therefore, that the first step in a reevaluation of materials would be to abandon the consideration of anything but sound and silence as the basic material of music.

When this is accomplished, music educators can begin to concentrate on process, the most vital abstraction of all. Process in this sense embraces all that one considers and acts upon in conceptualizing and knowing music. The underlying principles of the musical art are revealed to the student only through his or her active involvement with process. The skills and critical judgment necessary to the effective realization of music through composition and performance are learned by the student only through process. The capacity of the student to select, integrate, and use information in his or her daily problem-solving activity is developed through process. All else equal, the process-oriented person is better equipped to lead a life of intellectual growth and cultural refinement, a condition that leads to personal fulfillment, psychological stability, and a more complete awareness of the total art. Process,

> *W*hat exists as music in the public concert halls is becoming more and more unrelated to what exists as music in the schools; the two of these are totally unrelated to what exists as music in public communication.

therefore, must be the central activity of a music theory course; it must itself be the primary goal of learning. Once the talent and energy of youth find expression in a positive, imaginative, and highly skillful capacity to *do* in music, the prospects for the development and growth of a new music will be reasonably assured.

Part 3 of this series will offer a number of practical procedures that have proven successful in using creative problem-solving and related processes as the heart of a lower division theory program. These will, if properly used, serve as catalysts in the development of creative practices that are natural and stimulating to those involved.

In this article, Robert W. Sherman sets forth a philosophical basis for the practical application of approaches that can be used in providing a framework for creative development. He discusses four premises for establishing an atmosphere in which creativity can develop.

Creativity and the Condition of Knowing in Music

PART 3

by Robert W. Sherman

f an idea is to take root and prosper, it must be consumed as a seed by the mind of whoever accepts it and emerge again as a natural expression of his or her thoughts and actions. It is not only that the idea becomes part of the person, but also that the person becomes part of the idea.

If procedures are offered for fostering creativity, they can become useful to someone only when the basic principles that support the procedures are properly understood and each specific illustration is either modified or actually discarded. Each of the procedures to be presented in this article is subject, entirely or in part, to the following premises: (1) learning is best effected when a genuine need to know is present; (2) the exercise of imagination and originality by the inexperienced student is best achieved through his or her unfettered manipulation of unfamiliar materials; (3) technique as such is a natural consequence of experience gained in doing the very things for which the technique is needed; and (4) a genuine sense of proportion, artistry, and creative fulfillment requires that all problems in composition be complete and musically self-sufficient.

Robert W. Sherman is the former head of the Department of Music Theory and Composition, Ball State University, Muncie, Indiana. He is now retired and lives in Spring Hill, Florida. This article originally appeared in the December 1971 Music Educators Journal.

Unconventional Compositions

Students' first experience in a music theory class should lead them to a new awareness of sound. This is best achieved through the use of sound sources other than conventional instruments—sound sources that do not produce discrete pitches and do not submit to the organizing schemes peculiar to the tempered system. Students might be asked, at the very beginning of the course, to produce a composition of a particular duration using sounds produced on a specified number of commonly available metallic or wooden objects. The piece, when finished, could be presented as an improvisation by the composing student or played by several students from notation invented by the composer. An assignment of this type is easily accomplished by students, and though it might seem to be a simple-minded activity, it requires most of the behavior patterns related to creative processes used by any composer in the construction of music. Students must, of course, seek out the sound sources; they must experiment with a variety of ways to produce the sound, such as striking, rubbing, and dropping; they must contemplate each sound in terms of its individual characteristics and in terms of its relation to others; and finally, they must arrive at what they consider to be useful sound material. Each judgment made by the students is based on the nature of the material and their personal reactions to it. In order to allow students time for loosening up psychologically and to provide opportunities for experimenting with ideas that will contribute to the formation of technique, two or three assignments of this nature should be made. In practice, the instructor soon comes to an awareness of when a given activity is no longer profitable to students.

If possible, each of the "sound pieces" should be performed in class and discussed by the students. Though the discussions will necessarily be guided by the nature of what is produced, primary consideration should be given to whether the piece "works." If pieces are composed for a group of players, the composer's effectiveness in communicating through an invented notation would also be treated in discussion. Since the discussions will involve criticism, the class or the instructor might wish to present a few pertinent criteria to be considered or questions to be answered.

What might students learn from such an assignment? First, they will take the beginning step in the long process of understanding the act of composing. Their use of unfamiliar materials diminishes the possibility that they will be influenced by anything irrelevant to the problem. Beyond the primary functions of stimulating students' imaginations through creative activity and demonstrating the premise that technique evolves from the creative act itself, an assignment of this type can become the occasion for purposeful investigations into the nature of sound and the elementary principles of acoustics. When students try to invent a notation, they soon have to face the problem of communication; it is not long before they are compelled to consider the functions and limitations of notation. These problems can lead to readings about the evolution of notation, studies of new notation, and an appreciation of the role convention plays in the understanding of written music.

At this point, there are several directions in which a class might go, depending on the time available in the total program. It might pursue the sound studies further by constructing instruments and writing for them, by doing a few elementary projects in the electronic manipulation of concrete sounds, or by actually combining the two ideas into one. Projects of this type allow a more creative as well as practical approach to beginning studies in acoustics.

Making Compositions Work

Composing problems using discrete pitches and durations can begin with the construction of short monophonic pieces, each having a unique character, each being a complete piece, and each being written for an instrument in the class. It cannot be emphasized enough that expression, character, or whatever one wishes to call this aspect of musicality must precede and dominate the selection and function of materials and procedures in these as well as all future projects in creative problem-solving.

Also, the idea of conceiving music in terms of the qualities of an instrument and the capabilities of known players should be encouraged. Excepting a few cases, music is written for people to sing or play on something. These short pieces might begin with the student using alternating whole and half steps in conjunction with a limited number of durations. Similar schemes should be developed, eventually making use of all of the intervals in combinations that will function outside of the conventional diatonic systems. Also, the continued development of temporal relationships should be encouraged. The individual student's rhythmic sense should be the determining factor in the selection of these materials. These assignments require the class to investigate the characteristics of the instruments and to learn to spell intervals, to hear intervals, to transpose, to relate desired effects to notation, and to prepare music manuscript. Through this process, the student should begin to develop an awareness of melodic shape.

Though it is advantageous to begin with one line as suggested earlier, there is no particular reason why this way would have to be continued for as long as indicated. Multiple voices could be introduced, with the same general conditions prevailing, when it becomes apparent that the student is handling one line well. The term "multiple voices" should not be construed to mean four-part writing, the introduction of chordal writing, or any of the artificial systems that deal with past conventions. The student must now realize that a new dimension has been added to what constitutes a musical idea; he or she must become aware of texture and develop an understanding or feeling for the gestalt. What occurs between the voices must be arrived at by the same personal selection processes that determined the lines in the previous pieces. The same question must be answered again: Does the piece work? All this, of course, must be directed at expanding and refining the student's capacity to produce music in what will eventually evolve as a personal style.

The role of the instructor becomes increasingly difficult as the course progresses. The instructor must do all he or she can to assist the student in the development of a personal style without either suggesting an "anything goes" point of view or becoming too critical. It should be remembered that the essential difference between the student and the instructor is one of experience and whatever kind of "wisdom" attends it. The possibility exists, therefore, that in a given instance the student might be fundamentally more talented than the instructor and might easily solve a problem in composition in a manner at odds with the attending wisdom of the instructor's experience. Each party should, therefore, consider the plausibility of the other's point of view and move on whenever differences are strongly felt.

Increasing Complexity

Up to this point, students have been concerned entirely with what they and their classmates are creating. How long this should continue must be determined by how the class develops and the particular directions it happens to go in. If this type of instruction is used, no two classes will ever be the same; each will take on a structure and substance of its own. There is a point in the process when students can benefit from having various procedures substantiated and augmented through the analysis of other music. At no time, however, should students be encouraged to adopt the established composer's solution to problems. Analysis should serve to expand students' ideas, not replace them.

After the introduction of multiple voices, students should soon be ready to develop the processes by which they might expand their ideas into longer and more complex pieces. The various mechanical devices available for transforming and developing melodic material can be presented, used in a series of creative projects, and supported by analysis. Any

existing music can be used for this purpose, though the procedures are more obvious in the works of some composers than in those of others. The inherent possibilities for change effected by the use of any of the following devices, or combinations, are truly astronomical: transposition, inversion, retrograde, retrograde-inversion, interpolation, extension, deletion, octave displacement, interval expansion, interval contraction, fragmentation, rhythmic change, and "interversion." These are treated from an analytical point of view in Rudolph Reti's *The Thematic Process in Music* (New York: Macmillan, 1951).

By introducing the devices into the framework of the creative process, a number of problems may be created. When the ready mind is cast into a veritable supermarket of ideas, new controls must be exercised to prevent the kinds of excesses that will lead the student into an acceptance of gimmickry as the basis of the creative act. The introduction of discrete techniques of any sort invariably brings up the question of whether the composer is consciously aware of using them. The spirit in which the techniques should be introduced may be defined in part by the fact that all devices as such exist in music before they are described in language. There is also a basic, unavoidable callousness exercised by those who seek to isolate a unique feature from the complexity of the creative processes. Just as the student needs to recognize and exercise those techniques and procedures that lead to a capacity to perform music with freedom and lucidity, he or she must also recognize and exercise a variety of procedures related to the composing process. The student must, therefore, come to recognize that the desired end of all exercises of this type is the eventual freedom from concern for or conscious awareness of technique; that the terminology naming and isolating devices exists only for the purpose of verbal communication; and most important, that skill in using these devices does not in itself guarantee the creation of intelligible music. It might be said, however, that lack of such skill will certainly limit the composer's capacity to exploit a musical idea.

Keep It Simple

In presenting the concept of melodic transformation, the question of whether all devices should be presented at once might best be resolved by first discussing all of them to give an overview of the principle involved, and then by using them singly or in limited combinations in practice. Amid all the plenty, the student must develop a sense of propriety and economy in the use of these devices. The instructor's control over the situation can be exercised, without resorting to negative restrictions, by the design of the basic shapes and the selection of devices to be exploited. The student is thus able to function in a positive manner in the areas of his or her greatest needs.

Problems related to tonal and temporal organization and other formalizing factors will cause varying degrees of difficulty for each student in his or her expansion of melodic ideas. This should not be regarded as a fault, but as a logical consequence of processes geared to individualized learning. Though the general aims of a class will be singular, each student will develop personal mannerisms that will eventually lead him or her to a personalized expression of a principle shared by all. The instructor must diagnose problems in tonal and rhythmic organization and offer suggestions for refinement, and the student's concept of tonal organization should be expanded as well as refined. Concurrent with the work on melodic transformation, the student should cultivate the ability to frame and develop melodic ideas within a number of referential and nonreferential systems. The teacher should take care to see that the student does not confuse the principle of organization with the mannerisms of established composers. In dealing with the principle of serialized pitch, for example, the instructor should present the principle clearly and thoroughly so that the student does not confuse the principle with the personal application of it by a known composer. When students progress in the use of the principle and demonstrate a capacity to use it with some degree of success, they should then turn to analysis to broaden and refine their techniques. After each student has met with a number of organizing principles and has developed a capacity to conceive music

within a number of them, he or she should be encouraged to settle on one that best suits his or her temperament and natural abilities.

Harmony and Rhythm

One might ask why harmony is not used as the initial means of developing the student's creative abilities in composition. First, it is highly questionable that any composer would or could regard harmonic structure as the generating idea of a composition. This would be similar to a poet using grammar as the idea of a poem. Second, harmony, as a means of pitch orientation resulting from and representing tonal cohesion in music, is more of an organizing force and is related to "system" rather than "substance." Harmony, so conceived, is no more related to chords than to melody; therefore, chord structures and chordal relationships can be treated as manipulative substance. Concurrent with the student's work on melodic transformation, some attention should be given to the manipulation of sonority, texture, silence, dynamics, and all that can be developed in music.

Rhythmic problems should be handled in a manner similar to those related to harmony. Rhythm, having to do with the ordering of events in time, provides the means for making the comprehension of musical expression possible. Just as harmony should not be confused with the idea of vertical sonority, rhythm should not be confused with meter or pitch duration. Rhythm is the one overriding concern of the composer and performer alike: for each, it is his or her means of inflection, of establishing character, and ultimately, of shaping musical ideas into a musical gestalt. As in the case of harmony, rhythmic problems must be treated in terms of what students are trying to achieve and their degree of success in doing so. Also, as with harmony, students' rhythmic senses should be refined and expanded. The means to this end should again be a matter between the students and their materials; the introduction of established practices should not occur until students have at least partially solved their problems. The complex rhythmic interplay of melodic shapes, sonorities, dynamics, textures, and all the elements of a complete piece of music must develop as a natural, unselfconscious technical achievement of the student. When the means ("the process") is lost in the effect, "knowing" has been achieved and music has been composed. An undue awareness of the technical means used to achieve any musical effect is a certain indication of the failure of that means to succeed musically; it is an indication of the presence of gimmickry or the use of a device for its own sake. Consideration for harmonic and rhythmic organization is, therefore, a concern that permeates the total fabric of the class from the beginning, but does not serve as the generating force of either the class activities or the music that results.

> *At no time, however, should students be encouraged to adopt the established composer's solution to problems.*

The question of aural drill will not be dealt with in this article for three reasons. First, the kind of aural drill work generally used in the classroom is really not suited to this kind of instruction; second, the kind that would be advocated involves special equipment and programming that would require a great deal of explanation; and third, aural drill is a supportive process and, as such, would be outside the scope of this series. The teacher should realize, however, that the act of composing and the act of performing what has been composed are two class activities that contribute a great deal to the student's aural comprehension of music.

Other Projects

After students acquire a fair degree of competence in composition, a variety of long-term projects can be developed. For the most part, these can be accomplished outside class while activities related to analysis and other matters take place in class. One such project that has been most successful is the writing of commercials. In the space of sixty seconds, the student must make his or her point. He or she must produce something of character with concern for the psychological effect of the music. The use of speech, sound effects, possible electronic manipulation, and visual effects, if prepared for video, all contribute to one marvelous problem that is well defined in scope and open to the most demanding exercise of technique and imagination. Another successful project has been the cooperative composition of a short opera in which students write both the libretto and the music. A mixed-media project has involved the cooperative production of a film for which each student writes music. These and similar ventures have been presented in public performance. Some have been offered in composition forums and all have been performed in some fashion, if only in class. Individual projects, such as pieces for orchestra or wind ensemble, have been read by the university orchestra and band, and have occasionally been recorded.

On the surface, it might seem that the purpose of such a course is to make everyone a composer. In terms of what one considers a "composer" to be, we most certainly are not trying to make every student a composer; however, in the same sense that we attempt to make a performer of every student, we most certainly are. The success that performance has had among those who are not destined to be professional performers is the result of an atmosphere that leads such students to conduct themselves with the seriousness of intent expected of those who are to play professionally. This same success has been demonstrated repeatedly in the composition activity of the music theory classroom and has been the program's most effective contribution to the cultivation of student musicality.

Individual Creativity Can Be Increased

The creative activity described in this article represents a sampling of what occurs over a two-year period. This activity is supported by lecture, demonstration, analysis, discussion, performance, an electronic lab for drill in aural comprehension, a quantity of programmed materials, and a substantial library of reference books, anthologies, and scores in multiple copies.

There are ample studies to prove that creativity in an individual can be improved. It is also known that the learning that takes place through creative activity develops insights that lead to "knowing"—the most durable relationship one can establish with an idea.

What has been presented in this series is a kind of instruction that works. Necessary to this method is an outlook in which human ingenuity and drive are strong qualities that must be respected if effective learning is to take place. This type of instruction achieves the flexibility needed in dealing with the varied temperaments of students and demonstrates a faith in the talents and integrity of people. It seeks to restore the concept of the "complete musician."

Contributing to Our Heritage

A musical culture that is not attached to and does not thrive on the creative energies and products of its own people is sterile and lives only on what it can adopt from other cultures or retain from the past. The state of music in the university helps explain the state of music in the nation. The vast majority of our population is completely unaware of the existence in this country of a twentieth-century counterpart to what has come to be termed a "classical composer."

No one today would consider it desirable or even possible to have established a distinctly nationalistic music in the United States. We have, however, as have the other nations of the world, developed the international idiom so as to bear the unmistakable marks of our national temperaments. We do have a short-lived but highly significant musical heritage to which the creative among us contribute daily but the universities speak of rarely. The establishment of a fertile musical culture must begin at the university. The creative capacity of those who expect to teach must be developed to the fullest, and a new faith must be established in the artistic abilities of the young.

Section

Definition: Creativity—What Is It?

What is creativity? How is creativity defined in the context of models and processes? The following articles provide an excellent understanding of what creativity is and how it is defined.

In his article, Peter R. Webster takes a very broad and complex topic and provides a clearly understandable framework from which a working definition and understanding of creativity can be developed. He also develops the concept of incorporating musical creativity in the classroom and includes a means of evaluation. In addition to giving an excellent theoretical and clinical discussion of what creativity is, how it is defined, how it is assessed, and how it is conceptualized, Webster provides a useful annotated suggested readings list.

Creativity as Creative Thinking

by Peter R. Webster

There are few topics in music teaching and learning that are as fundamentally important as creativity. From the earliest works of Lowell Mason to the latest publications by MENC, thousands of words have been written about this subject. It has influenced the forming of philosophy, the writing of goals and objectives, and the design of countless lesson plans. The *Music Educators Journal* alone has accounted for more than twenty articles since 1960. One bibliography of literature that deals with creativity in music education contains over a hundred annotated citations organized into theoretical, practical, and empirical categories.[1]

Much of this literature focuses on practice. Important monographs on creative teaching have been written, including books on traditional composition techniques as well as unusual approaches. Many of the major texts on teaching practice deal directly with creative strategies. For a listing of some of the materials, see the "Suggested Readings."

In terms of student outcomes, approaches such as those of Carl Orff and Emile Jaques-Dalcroze stress

Peter R. Webster is an associate professor of music education at Northwestern University, Evanston, Illinois. Actively involved in teaching and research on children's creative thinking in music, he has developed approaches to the measurement of creative thinking in music through informal composition and computer simulation. This article originally appeared in the May 1990 Music Educators Journal.

certain kinds of creative activity. The Contemporary Music Project and the Manhattanville Music Curriculum Project, two well-known efforts of the 1960s, contained detailed descriptions of creative strategies as a central focus of curriculum design. The Ann Arbor Symposium II and the Suncoast Music Education Forum are examples of professional meetings that have dealt exclusively with this topic.[2]

Continued Confusion

Although much of this work has been helpful in understanding the complexities of creativity and in helping to formulate practice, confusion continues about just what the word means. For instance, a ten-year-old child's Sunday piano recital might be termed a milestone of creativity by some, while others might view the same child's Orff improvisation during Monday's music class in the same terms. Some view the very presence of music in the schools as an example of educational commitment to creativity, while others gauge creativity solely by the products of these programs or by the awards they win. Some regard creativity as a term best reserved for geniuses, while others look to the spontaneous songs of the three-year-old or the daydreams of the adolescent.

Many questions about creativity continue to prevail. Is creativity product, or process, or both? Should it be considered primarily something that takes place in composition? Can it be readily measured? Does it have anything to do with music aptitude? Isn't it the same as intelligence? Isn't it really only a "general music" activity? Can it be taught? There remains little doubt about the importance of creativity in the music education profession, but little collective sense of what it is.

New Thinking

Music educators and psychologists interested in artistic development have recently supplied answers to these and many other questions. Many of their studies are based, in part, on a more focused view of creativity—one that centers on the *mental processes* associated with creative production. One of the main problems we face is the word "creativity" itself. It has been used in so many different contexts that it has lost much of its meaning and power, especially in terms of music and children. In the educational context, it might be more prudent to use the term "creative thinking." There are a number of reasons for this.

By focusing on creative thinking, we place the emphasis on the process itself and on its role in music teaching and learning. We are challenged to seek answers to how the mind works with musical material to produce creative results.[3] This approach demystifies creativeness, places it in context with other kinds of abilities and external influences, and—perhaps most important—makes our job as educators much clearer.

There are four characteristics of the recent literature on creative thinking that are worthy of consideration: it shows (1) an emphasis on the role of musical imagination or musical imagery, (2) theoretical modeling of the creative process, (3) new approaches to the measurement of creative aptitude, and (4) systematic observation of creative behavior, often in natural settings. A fifth characteristic is now emerging: the use of computers and sound technology as tools for recording and stimulating creative thought. Each of these

characteristics has important implications for practice and each helps in its own way to clarify what we really mean by the term "creativity."

Musical Imagination

The mind's ability to "think in sound" has been an important issue for musical achievement for some time. For example, a private trumpet teacher might encourage a student to "hear" a musical line internally before playing it to improve the quality of

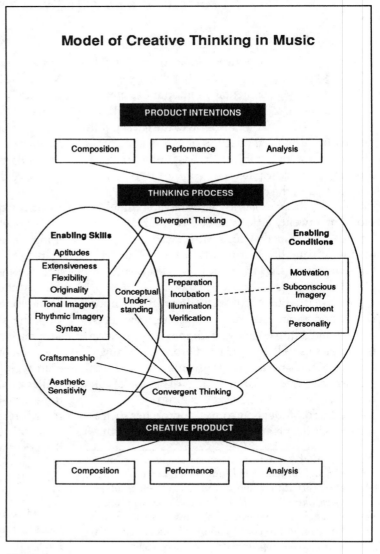

Figure 1.

performance. A general music specialist can often encourage a sixth grade class to "remember" a musical passage during a listening lesson in order to compare the passage to an occurrence later. Conducting teachers encourage students to "imagine" the sound of a score before rehearsal.

This ability to internally imagine sound meaningfully is not only important for music achievement and *convergent* tasks (tasks designed to yield a single right answer), but is also critical for creative thinking ability and specifically for *divergent* tasks (tasks for which several answers are possible). What is of interest is the encouragement of imaginative, divergent thinking in the classroom, rehearsal hall, and private studio. Typical questions and statements that encourage this kind of thinking are:

"Imagine how the composer might have changed the ending to sound more tentative. How could this be done?"

"Think of what it would sound like without the strings—with just the tuba and piccolo playing together."

"Can you think of another accompaniment pattern for that melody? Play it for me."

"Clarinets, imagine what that fugue subject would sound like if it had been written a century later."

It is this kind of imaginative problem-solving with musical sound that plays such an important role in the creative process and that has captured the attention of many music professionals interested in the formal study of creativity. Ironically, it is precisely this kind of thinking that is so often not stressed by music teachers—often ignored in favor of factual or skill-oriented content. Factual information is, of course, critical for imaginative thinking, but we must provide students with opportunities for applying this conceptual understanding in creative tasks. It is equally ironic that mathematics or history teachers might be more effective in getting students to think imaginatively about their subjects than is the music teacher.

Model of the Creative Process

How does this imaginative thinking relate to the big picture? Figure 1 shows one view of the creative thinking process. Such attempts at conceptual modeling are useful for teachers and researchers. They suggest relationships that imply possible teaching strategy and give direction to research. They can also generate a platform for debate in the profession—always a healthy sign. This model is designed to be representative of creative thinking by both children and adults, although certain aspects of the model might be qualitatively different at various stages of development.[4]

Product intention. Composition, performance/improvisation, and analysis (written and listening) can be considered at the outset of creative thinking as goals or "intentions" of the creator. At the same time, they represent the final product of creation. The product intentions of school-age children are usually limited under our current educational system to performance/improvisation and listening, a fact that, I hope, will change as schools encourage more written composition and analysis. Each product intention results in subtle differences during the creative process, but the inner workings of the process are probably quite similar. An important point for music education is that creative thinking is part of the total curriculum effort and should not be viewed as just a classroom activity.

Enabling skills. With the intention established, the creator must rely on a set of skills that allow for the thinking process to occur. These skills form the basis of a musical intelligence and interact with the thinking process in a rich variety of ways.

First among these skills is the necessary collection of *musical aptitudes.* These are individual skills that are subject to influence by the environment during the early years of development and possibly into early adult life. They include such convergent thinking skills as the ability to recognize rhythmic and tonal patterns and musical syntax (sensitivity to the musical whole). Certain divergent, imaginative skills are also critical, such as musical extensiveness (the amount of time invested in creative imaging), flexibility (the range of musical expression in terms of dynamics, tempo, and pitch), and originality (unusualness of expression). These musical aptitudes are largely innate, although they are subject to developmental improvement with training.

Another enabling skill is conceptual understanding: the *knowledge of facts* that constitute the substance of musical understanding. Furthermore, the possession of two more types of ability fall into this category: *craftsmanship* (the ability to apply factual knowledge in the service of a complex musical task) and *aesthetic sensitivity* (the ability to shape sound structures to capture the deepest levels of personal feeling—an ability that is demonstrated over the full length of a musical work).

Conceptual understanding, craftsmanship, and aesthetic sensitivity obviously grow with age and experience, but transfer of these abilities into the mosaic of creative thinking does not often occur naturally. This transfer might well be an important goal of formal music education.

Enabling conditions. In addition to the personal skills that drive the creative thinking process, there are a number of variables involved that are *not* musical. These influences vary greatly from person to person and mingle with musical skills in delicate and complicated ways.

One of these, *motivation*, comprises those drives (both external and internal) that help keep the creator on task. Another, *subconscious imagery*, is the presence of mental activity that occurs quite apart from the conscious mind and that may help to inform the creative process during times when the creator is occupied consciously with other concerns.

Another, *personality*, describes factors such as risktaking, spontaneity, openness, perspicacity, sense of humor, and preference for complexity that seem to exist in many creative people and that may hold some significance for enabling the creative process. *Environment* is the host of characteristics that define the creator's working conditions and contribute to the creative process, including financial support, family conditions, musical instruments, acoustics, media, societal expectations, peer pressure, and many others.

Thinking process in the central core. The center of the model in figure 1 indicates movement, in stages, between divergent and convergent thinking. These stages involve time to play with ideas (preparation), time to have away from the tasks (incubation), and time to work in structured ways through the ideas (verification) after solutions have presented themselves (illumination). A very important implication

for music teaching is that we must allow enough time for creative thinking to occur.

There are a number of important connections between this process and the enabling skills and conditions. Of the musical aptitudes, some (those of tonal and rhythmic imagery and musical syntax) are most clearly connected to convergent thinking. Tonal and rhythmic imagery concern the ability to perceive sound in relation to change and involve the representation of sound in memory. Musical syntax is the ability to shape musical expressions in a logical manner according to patterns of musical repetition, contrast, and sequencing. In this sense, a grasp of syntax is closely related to aesthetic sensitivity and is an early indication of this skill before extensive formal training. The aptitudes of extensiveness, flexibility, and originality are clearly connected to divergent thinking. Conceptual understanding directly affects both divergent and convergent thinking. (Divergent thinking requires the mind to survey its data banks for possible musical content, so the more that is in those banks, the better. It is impossible to expect individuals to think creatively if nothing is there with which to think creatively!) Craftsmanship and aesthetic sensitivity are also connected to convergent thinking because they require careful manipulation of musical material in sequential ways. Divergency is directly related to aesthetic sensitivity as well.

Another major implication shown in this model for music teaching is the idea that environments that encourage divergent thinking in music are just as important as environments that encourage convergency of thought. Are we doing enough in our rehearsals, private studios, and classrooms to insure the very heart of this model?

Measures of Creative Aptitude

Only recently have attempts to actually measure creative aptitude in music begun. Much of this work has focused on young children, ages six to ten, and has sought to identify divergent and convergent thinking skills in music using musical tasks in gamelike contexts. For example, a measure I developed uses an amplified voice, a round sponge ball with a piano, and a set of temple blocks to engage children in musical imagery.[5] The tasks begin very simply and progress to higher levels of difficulty in terms of divergent thinking. There are no right or wrong answers to the tasks.

The first section of this evaluation procedure is designed to help the children become familiar with the instruments used and how they are arranged. The children explore the parameters of "high/low," "fast/slow," and "loud/soft" in this section and throughout the measure. The way they manipulate these parameters is, in turn, used as one of the bases for scoring. They are given tasks that involve images of rain in a water bucket, magical elevators, and the sounds of trucks.

The middle section asks the children to engage in more challenging activities with the

What is happening in this picture?
(child responds)
Can you show me with your hand the way a frog moves?
(child responds)
Using this sponge ball on the piano, can you make up some frog music that begins soft and, little by little, gets louder and louder?
(child responds)
Now can you make some smooth, rolling sounds with the ball?
(child responds)

Great! Now it's time to make some more frog music! I would like you to make up a piece of music that has jumpy sounds and smooth sounds, soft and loud sounds, and fast and slow sounds. Feel free to use all the keys on the piano and to make your piece as long as you want. Now think about your frog music for a while and when you think you're ready, I would like to hear about it.
(child responds)

The administrator should move to the rear and to the side of the child during performance so that the child will not be tempted to seek approval from the administrator for the various parts of the composition.
After this task is finished, proceed immediately to the concluding set of tasks by placing the first space picture on the piano music stand.

Figure 2. Administrator's instructions (illustration from Measure of Creative Thinking in Music)

instruments and to focus on the creation of music using each of the instruments singly. Children enter into a kind of musical question/answer dialogue with the mallet and temple blocks, and they create songs with the round ball on the piano and with the voice and the microphone. They use images that include the concept of "frog" music (accomplished by hopping and rolling the ball on the piano) and that of a robot singing in the shower (realized with the child's voice through the microphone).

In the last section of the procedure, the children are encouraged to use multiple instruments in tasks whose settings are less structured. They tell a space story in sounds, using drawings as a visual aid. The final task asks the children to create a composition that uses all the instruments and that has a beginning, a middle, and an end.

This measure and others like it yield scores for such factors as musical originality, extensiveness, and flexibility, as well as musical syntax. Measurement strategies are based on the careful analysis of videotapes or audiotapes of children actually engaged in the activities. Objective criteria as well as rating scales are used: Musical extensiveness, for example, is measured by the time involved in the creative tasks, while evaluators rate originality by observing the manner in which pitch, tempo, and dynamics are manipulated.

Results based on administration of the test to over three hundred children have been encouraging.

Reliability and validity data seem to suggest that the children's responses follow consistent patterns and that the content of the tasks is appropriate. The tasks are not measuring the same skills as traditional musical aptitude tests (which measure tonal and rhythmic imagery), nor are they related with any statistical degree of significance to general intelligence. The scores on the tests do not seem to be grouped according to differences in sex, race, or socioeconomic background.

Perhaps the most important point surrounding this work, however, is that what was once thought to be unapproachable and mysterious is now being studied. The actual tasks in these measures also serve as models for music teaching strategy as educators seek to engage children in imaginative thinking about music. (See figure 2.)

Observation

Some of the most interesting writing in recent times has come from studies that have systematically observed the products and processes of children's creative expression in music and have attempted to analyze what happens as children create. The aim is to provide a sense of how the mind represents sound at various stages in development and how the music educator might benefit from this knowledge. Strategies involve engaging children in either compositional, improvisatory, or quasi-improvisatory tasks; recording the results; and then studying the characteristics of the music the children produce. Unlike efforts that are designed to create a standardized measure as described above, these studies essentially describe content as it is happening.[6]

We already see some interesting trends. Until children are five or six, their rhythmic and melodic material is somewhat idiosyncratic, with no predictable pattern. It is not clear if this is because of motor coordination problems in the production of sounds or it is a true representation of the children's inner hearing. After this age, both rhythmic and melodic structures seem to be more predictable. Between the ages of six and ten, changing or mixed meters occur, giving way to quite consistent patterns after age ten. Duple meter seems to be preferred by most older children.

After age fix or six, consistent melodic and tonal characteristics also become more pronounced. The music of six- to ten-year-old children exhibits a gradual development of feeling for cadence structures and a growing awareness of tonal center within melodies. It seems clear that as children imitate the songs in their environment, their own music is influenced accordingly. After the age of ten, children become much more conscious of "correctness" of musical structure and tend to create music that is more organized in terms of rules, but not necessarily more original.

There seems to be a general increase in the use of both rhythmic and melodic motives from age five to eleven. Interest in the actual musical development of a melodic motive rises as children reach age eleven, but rhythmic development seems to remain relatively unchanged at all levels.

Much of this information is preliminary and more careful study is needed. What is most important for music education is the fact that there seem to be patterns of thinking and behavior that can be studied. By asking children to solve musical problems with the goal of creating a musical product, we have an opportunity to learn more about the creative process while at the same time engaging children in tasks that are fundamental to music as art.

Technology: Its Future Role

Musical imagination, conceptual modeling, measurement, and observation are four keys to a better understanding of creative thinking in music. Each of these keys stands to gain measurably from technology. Much has been said about computers, electronic keyboards, software, and MIDI as teaching tools for convergent goals in music education. It is *not*, however, with this kind of education that such technology holds its greatest promise. It is rather with the encouragement and careful study of divergent, imaginative musical thinking.

Imagine a child seated at a music keyboard with a computer screen providing the score. This child composes a brief fragment of music by playing on the music keyboard. This fragment is displayed on the screen (in traditional notation or in other forms) and is played through speakers. The child continues to expand the fragment, working with many different timbres, additional voices, dynamics, and phrase patterns. At one point the child becomes frustrated and quits, saving the work in a file. The child returns later to the saved composition and continues work until a final version is ready to be shared with the teacher and the class. The child then prints a copy of the score and takes it home for the refrigerator door, and the teacher transfers the recording to cassette tape for the child's parents to hear. Throughout the entire process, the computer has saved every moment of the child's work and can "replay" the "electronic sketches" in exacting detail. Although this is of little interest to the child, it is of great interest to the teacher, who can use these electronic sketches to evaluate the student's progress. Indeed, Harvard University's Project Zero uses teacher review of similar "portfolios" of student work as a basis for evaluation (see Lyle Davidson's article in this book.)

Just a few years ago, such a scenario would have seemed financially and technologically out of the question. Not so today. With software and hardware to support multimedia applications, music workstations of this sort now exist in music labs in several schools. Similar projects will be easily designed by the teacher for performers and listeners as well. This technology will soon help us to expand our understanding of musical imagination, to challenge our concepts of the creative process, and to measure and observe creative thinking in ways never thought possible. The real question is, will we be able to take advantage of this power?

Providing the Answers

Creative thinking, then, is a dynamic mental process that alternates between divergent (imaginative) and convergent (factual) thinking, moving in stages over time. It is enabled by internal musical skills and outside conditions and results in a final musical product that is new for the creator. Focusing on creative thinking is an important beginning to our understanding of creativity and may yield important answers to the questions raised at the beginning of this article.

A child's potential for creative thinking is not so complex that it cannot be measured and should be considered as part of an expanded view of traditional musical aptitude. It is not the same as general intelligence or musical achievement skill. Composition is not the only end product of the creative thinking process. Performances of precomposed music, improvisation, and careful listening and analysis all involve the creative thinking process. The rehearsal hall, the private studio, and the classroom are all sites for such thinking. Creative thinking can be taught by providing children with chances to explore musical images and by applying them in problem-solving tasks. Technology may play an important role in our teaching strategy.

In the final analysis, we are limited only by our own creative thinking as teachers. Exciting the imagination of our children about music is what it is all about. Facts and skills will not do it alone.

Notes

1. Peter R. Webster. "Creative Thinking in Music: Approaches to Research," in *Music Education in the United States: Contemporary Issues*, ed. Terry Gates (Tuscaloosa: University of Alabama Press, 1988), 66–81.

2. *Documentary Report of the Ann Arbor Symposium on the Applications of Psychology to the Teaching and Learning of Music: Session III* (Washington, DC: Music Educators National Conference, 1983); *Proceedings from the Suncoast Music Education Forum on Creativity* (Tampa, FL: Department of Music, University of South Florida, 1989).

3. This approach is in line with current work in music cognition and is part of a larger effort in the social and behavioral sciences, neurosciences, and computer science. For a general overview, see Howard Gardner, *The Mind's New Science* (New York: Basic Books, 1987).

4. For a fuller description of this model, see Peter R. Webster, "Conceptual Bases for Creative Thinking in Music," in *Music and Child Development*, ed. J. Craig Peery, Irene Peery, and Thomas Draper (New York: Springer-Verlag, 1987), 158–74.

5. Peter R. Webster, "Refinement of a Measure of Creative Thinking in Music," in *Applications of Research in Music Behavior*, ed. Clifford Madsen and Carol Prickett (Tuscaloosa: University of Alabama Press, 1987), 257-71.

6. For an excellent review of this literature, see John Kratus, "A Time Analysis of the Compositional Processes Used by Children Ages 7 to 11," *Journal of Research in Music Education* 37, no. 1 (Spring 1989): 5-20.

Suggested Readings

Balkin, Alfred. "The Creative Music Classroom: Laboratory for Creativity in Life." *Music Educators Journal* 71, no. 5 (January 1985): 43-46. This article presents several practical suggestions for creative activities in teaching music. The author stresses that teachers move away from "yessing" (always expecting children to supply the one correct answer) and toward discovery learning. Encouraging children to make guesses about musical problems is stressed.

Bennett, Stan. "Learning to Compose: Some Research, Some Suggestions." *Journal of Creative Behavior* 9, no. 3 (Summer 1975): 205-10. Bennett suggests approaches to teaching composition based upon his study of professional composers and his experiences as a composer. Having discovered that a germinal idea is often the first stage of composition and that this is often developed through improvisation, Bennett proposes an improvisational approach built on the immersion process by which language is acquired.

Benson, Warren. CMP 4: *Creative Projects in Musicianship*. Washington, DC: Music Educators National Conference, 1967. This volume, the fourth in a series of MENC publications about the Contemporary Music Project (CMP), summarizes projects sponsored by CMP at two locations: Ithaca College and the Interlochen Arts Academy. The book describes each project briefly and concludes with some general observations about teaching "creative-process" courses in music.

———. "The Creative Child Could Be Any Child." *Music Educators Journal* 59, no. 8 (April 1973): 38-40. This article provides excellent tips on how to evaluate the products of students' creative thinking. Benson urges questions such as: "Did the piece interest us?" "Were there any obvious flaws?" "What would you do to correct the trouble spots?" He makes the point that each student should be encouraged to enjoy the pursuit of creativity and not just understand the procedures or rules for composition in creating a song.

Burns, Mary. "Musical Creative Learning and Problem Solving." *The Creative Child and Adult Quarterly* 11, no. 4 (1986): 234-40. Burns presents a case for the need to include creative activities in the general music curriculum. The Kodály and Orff approaches are cited as appropriate avenues for this approach. A lesson plan is presented for the composition of a song based on the creation of a haiku. The lesson is quite specific as to the musical content of the creative process and as to the steps taken in the classroom to make the lesson work smoothly.

Cheyette, Irving. "Developing the Innate Musical Creativity of Children." *Journal of Creative Behavior* 11, no. 4 (Fall 1977): 256-60. This article gives some guidelines for teachers in developing creativity through a project that includes creating a story and the accompanying music. Cheyette argues that children must develop a background of enriched sensory images and presents ways to accomplish this. A list of teacher activities is provided.

Cheyette, Irving, and Herbert Cheyette. *Teaching Music Creatively in the Elementary School*. New York: McGraw-Hill, 1969. A textbook for potential music teachers, this volume approaches the teaching of music from the assumption that the best way to learn music is to make music. In addition to chapters on developing an awareness of the musical elements, it also offers information on developing a classroom orchestra with informal instruments and on developing the innate creativity of children.

Dennis, Brian. "Experimental Music in Schools." *International Society for Music Education Jour-*

nal 2 (1972): 10-21. The article puts forth the idea that we should think less about teaching the music of the past and consider music of today as an important part of the music we teach. Dennis argues for a better communication between composers of the present and their audiences. Children's performance of contemporary music by established composers is encouraged; examples are given.

Feinberg, Saul. "Creative Problem-Solving and the Music Listening Experience." *Music Educators Journal* 61, no. 1 (September 1974): 53-59. Feinberg argues for a new approach to listening based on a model that stresses both a problem-solving approach and a knowledge-based approach. Ideas for music listening lessons are presented based on the general factors of fluency, flexibility, and elaboration of thought. The author also makes a connection between procedures for teaching listening and the overall creative process. The article also provides the underlying theme that such an approach is closely associated with aesthetic education goals.

Galloway, Margaret. "Let's Make an Opera: A Happening with 120 Young Children." *Journal of Creative Behavior* 6, no. 1 (Winter 1972): 41-48. The article describes how the story "Peter Pan" was produced as an opera by students; it is an example of student creativity in original composition, dialogue writing, set making, and involvement in practically every other aspect of production.

Hoenack, Peg. "Unleash Creativity—Let Them Improvise." *Music Educators Journal* 57, no. 9 (May 1971): 33-36. As a foundation for creativity, this article discusses several methods of improvisation in the music class using whatever instruments or rhythm accessories are available. Development of these skills in the early grades supports the art of composing and listening as a child learns to communicate with others.

Holderried, Elizabeth Swist. "Creativity in My Classroom." *Music Educators Journal* 55, no. 7 (March 1969): 37-39. Holderried describes how Edgard Varèse's *Ionisation* and *Poème électronique* served as the stimuli for a creative project in her general music classes. Children suggested various approaches and were included in every phase of

the project, which included performances of their works.

Lasker, Henry. *Teaching Creative Music in Secondary Schools.* Boston: Allyn and Bacon, 1971. This book deals with techniques for acquainting children with the process of music composition, specifically for stimulating the ideas and climate for composition. There are many musical examples and suggestions.

Marsh, Mary. *Explore and Discover Music: Creative Approaches to Music Education in Elementary, Middle, and Junior High Schools.* New York: Macmillan, 1970. This book is based on the premise that it is essential to find more creative ways of teaching music in order to develop the creative potential of each student. Marsh advocates a teaching process in which the teacher organizes activities so that the student discovers the concepts of music as he or she is involved in the activity. Specific teaching strategies and examples of how various students react to the activities of these strategies are given.

Paynter, John. *Music in the Secondary School Curriculum—Trends and Development in the Classroom.* New York: Cambridge University Press, 1982. This book offers extensive information on establishing a music curriculum that centers on creative thinking skills. An excellent list of contemporary scores and recordings is included, together with examples of course organization.

Pogonowski, Lenore. "Bridging the Gap from the Podium to the General Music Class Using Concert Percussion." In *Music in the High School*, edited by Timothy Gerber and William O. Hughes, 55-63. Reston, VA: Music Educators National Conference, 1988. This article provides an approach for teaching music to high school general music students. It allows the student to be actively involved and socially interactive in the classroom by performing, composing, improvising, conducting, and evaluating music. Concert percussion instruments are used because of their accessibility and ease of use by those not able to read music. Specific strategies for implementation are included.

Regelski, Thomas, "A Sound Approach to Sound Composition." *Music Educators Journal* 72, no. 9 (May 1986): 41-45. This article contains a rationale for including sound composition activities in a music curriculum and gives concrete suggestions as to the implementation of these activities. Models of action learning, activities approach, and problem-solving skills in music are also given.

Ristad, Eloise. A *Soprano on Her Head: Right-Side-Up Reflections of Life and Other Performances*. Moab, Utah: Real People Press, 1982. This book challenges traditional music teaching with new insights for dealing with problems in music performance. Ristad suggests gaining control by letting go, achieving excellence by not trying, practicing through imagery, and learning by simple awareness.

Schafer, R. Murray. *Creative Music Education*. New York: Schirmer Books, 1979. This book was originally published as five separate booklets: *The Composer in the Classroom, Ear Cleaning, The New Soundscape, When Words Sing*, and *The Rhinoceros in the Classroom*. The author, a Canadian composer, describes some dialogues that he has held with elementary, high school, and first-year university students. Examples of music lessons covering the topics of noise, silence, tone, timbre, and texture are included.

Thackray, Rupert. *Creative Music in Education*. London: Novello and Company, 1965. This volume begins with a justification for creative activities in the schools: "The aim of this book is to suggest possible ways of approach for teachers and students at all levels from primary school to the college." Thackray includes sections on vocal improvisation, instrumental improvisation, and composition, and endorses the Orff approaches. The book contains a number of practical suggestions for engaging children in creative activities.

Thompson, Keith P. "Vocal Improvisation for Elementary Students." *Music Educators Journal* 66, no. 5 (January 1980): 69-71. Thompson argues that creating music should be included in the general music curriculum because it allows the students to learn about aspects of music in a personal way. The act of creating music allows the students to exercise cognitive and affective decision-making processes. A three-stage process of creativity is proposed. Vocal improvisation is the recommended medium for exercising the creative pro-

cess, and a series of activities using the author's creative process is given.

Thoms, Hollis. "Encouraging the Musical Imagination through Composition." *Music Educators Journal* 73, no. 5 (January 1987): 27-30. Thoms describes three projects involving high-school-age students in the composition process: compositions centered on theme and variation form, musical setting of a poem, and a multimedia event with a focus on the musical concept of "line."

Welwood, Arthur. "Improvising with Found Sounds." *Music Educators Journal* 66, no. 5 (January 1980): 72-77. Welwood argues that composing and improvising should be as routine as writing an English composition or learning the multiplication tables. The goal of these activities in the classroom is not to master the art of composition but to become involved in the creative selection and arrangement of musical materials and to develop skills in self-evaluation along with constructive self-criticism. "Found" instruments are any ready-made objects that are capable of producing sound: They may be of materials such as glass, plastic, or paper. Many performance possibilities are available to an individual or an orchestra. This concept will expand the student's attitude toward twentieth-century music and the music of non-Western cultures.

Wiggins, Jacqueline H. "Composition as a Teaching Tool." *Music Educators Journal* 75, no. 8 (April 1989): 35-38. Wiggins lists many benefits of compositional activities, including an increase in innate creative thinking in children, encouraging pride in their musicianship, and the reinforcement of the meaning of musical concepts. Three lesson plans are presented, each devoted to either individual, small-group, or large-group instruction.

Williams, Polly. "Musical Creativity: An Interdisciplinary Approach from Troy to Carthage from Vergil to Berlioz." *Creative Child and Adult Quarterly* 2, no. 3 (1977): 148-50. Williams provides curricular suggestions for the use of grand opera in developing various forms of musical creativity among a range of age-groups. The author describes ways in which music and subjects such as literature, dance, history, psychology, and the visual arts may be linked through interdisciplinary studies built around opera.

Alfred Balkin offers the reader an easily understandable definition of creativity. In a nontheoretical, nonclinical manner and drawing on several sources, he describes the characteristics and qualities of a creative individual. Using "the creativity equation, C = 3P" (creativity = person, process, and product), Balkin provides descriptive lists and clear definitions that will further assist readers in their conceptual understanding of creativity.

What Is Creativity?
What Is It Not?

by Alfred Balkin

What is creativity?
What is it not?
Do some possess little,
And others a lot?

Even the experts
Tend to agree
On traits found in common
To a certain degree.

What are some of the commonalties found in creative people? For there to be genuine growth and interaction between classroom music teachers and their students, it is essential to put creativity in some rational, attainable, conceptual perspective; to discard the mystique; to explain what creativity is and is not; and to describe conditions or attitudes that nurture its proliferation.

The word "creativity" seems to turn many people off, particularly, strange as it may seem, people involved in the arts. In truth, it *is* overused, misused, confused, abused, and generally misunderstood. The word tends to lose meaning because it is often used indiscriminately, but if used in an enlightened

Alfred Balkin is a professor of education, a composer, and the coordinator of the Integrated Creative Arts Program in the College of Education at Western Michigan University, Kalamazoo. This article originally appeared in the May 1990 Music Educators Journal.

manner, it can have considerable meaning and application. Just what is this mysterious quality called creativity? Many people find it fascinating and believe that those who are creative are in an exclusive club that does not initiate new members.

First and foremost, creativity is *not* a synonym for talent. True talent is a gift—ephemeral, elusive, undefinable, unteachable, unlearnable. In the film *Amadeus*, Salieri despondently and jealously described Mozart's genius in such terms. Creativity, on the other hand, is an acquired behavior—learnable, teachable, tangible, and crucial to human development. The talented person may be, and often is, creative. The creative person may be, but less often is, talented. Creativity and talent are not equivalent. The creative person makes things happen; the talented person might. When a person possesses both qualities, however, great things may be in store. Creative behavior may enable a person to discover a long-dormant talent. Many such people have established themselves not only in the arts and sciences but in all fields. The continuation of such creative behaviors has allowed talents to grow and flourish. For some, this transformation may have been initiated in music class, and fortunately for today's schoolchildren, that possibility remains strong.

Seeing Connections

Before delving more deeply into what creativity is, it should be duly noted that intelligent people are not necessarily creative. There is no absolute correlation between high IQ and a high level of creativity. Creative people, however, *are* generally quite intelligent. These points have been clearly enunciated and amply supported by research that is cited in George Kneller's *The Art and Science of Creativity* (New York: Holt, Rinehart and Winston, 1967).

You may be familiar with something I call "the creativity equation," $C = 3P$. Obviously, the "C" refers to creativity, and you may have guessed that one of the three Ps refers to "person"—the cornerstone of the creative process. But what is creativity?

Simply stated, to create means to do, and that is the key. Creative people do things. They make. They assemble. They put together. They make connections where connections were not previously apparent. Of course, such connections existed, but it took the creative person's perception to discern their existence and bring them to light. You may have heard the old real estate adage, "The three most important things to consider in buying real estate are location, location, and location." For thinking about creativity, it's connections, connections, and connections. There are many other factors, but this is the nucleus. What is composing all about, if not connections?

Creativity is often mistakenly used as a synonym for originality, though creative behavior usually has elements of originality. It is similarly misused as a synonym for spontaneity, which may, in many instances, refer to attention-seeking, flamboyant, possibly dangerous, or bizarre behavior as opposed to creative enterprise. Oscar Wilde's walking down a London street with a rose clutched between his teeth would certainly qualify as bizarre, or at least a bit strange. Although Wilde was both a talented and creative writer, the aforementioned behavior would be inappropriately noncreative, though perhaps not in the same league with a rock star's nightly destruction of his $3,000 guitar on stage—for effect and to "protest" our value system. The fact that the star earns $100,000 per concert through our value system makes it easier to replace the trashed instruments.

Making a Contribution

I have joined those who associate creativity with achievement. If a person is doing something that, at least in intent if not realization, will contribute to society, he or she is being creative. One could make the case that doing something good for oneself is, in a sense, contributing to one's mental health, and thereby contributing to society. Is that stretching the point, or is it simply making a connection? Perhaps stretching the point (as well as the imagination) is precisely how connections are made. Making a contribution to society is what immediately sets a creative person apart from one who is merely original or spontaneous. There is no societal caveat attached to originality or spontaneity, both of which, if used toward creative ends, are highly desirable, constructive, and sought-after attributes. Used toward socially unacceptable or evil ends, they can be destructive forces, as history shows.

Many creative people, such as comic actor Robin Williams or television host Oprah Winfrey, *are* clever, witty, and original, but original, spontaneous, and clever people are not necessarily creative. They don't produce. Ultimately, society, right or wrong, rewards or rejects the creative person only for the *products* that emerge from the creative *process*. If they like the products, they accept the person, even when that person demonstrates antisocial behaviors. Yes, I did emphasize products and process. The three Ps of the creativity equation are now all on the table: person, process, and product. Creativity, then, is an interaction of a person or persons with a process to produce a product. Sometimes the product is the personality itself. Sometimes the product may be the solution to a problem, which is also, in a sense, a product. This brings us back to our key—the creative person.

> *Choices, alternatives,*
> *failures, and doubt:*
> *The creative person*
> *works all of them out.*

Finding Answers

There is general agreement among practitioners, theorists, and writers dealing with the nature of creativity as to what characteristics may be attributed to the creative person. These qualities have been especially well delineated by Don Koberg and Jim Bagnall in *The Universal Traveler* (Los Altos, CA: William Kaufmann, Inc., 1972) and by George Kneller in *The Art and Science of Creativity*. I have combined and synthesized their checklists and have editorialized on some points. According to these writers, the creative person is:

- a dealer in options (the jazz improviser)
- a logical problem solver, but also one who can appreciate that something illogical can make sense (the perceptive teacher)
- a habit-breaker
- a constructively discontented person—in Piagetian terms, he or she is in a nearly constant state of disequilibrium; somehow, the person has to be dissatisfied with things as they stand
- a divergent or off-the-wall thinker as well as a convergent or rational thinker
- innovative
- intelligent (all good teachers)
- aware in a heightened way, noticing what others do not (the great conductor)
- fluent and often verbally articulate, producing more ideas on a subject than the ordinary person
- original, giving birth to ideas that are statistically infrequent for the population and that represent remoteness of association
- often skeptical
- confident, if not fearless.

The creative person also:
- enjoys being off-center
- works with steady, unrelenting, unremitting obsession
- is intellectually "playful" and able to see the humorous side of a situation as a necessary emotional release (what every classroom music teacher should be)
- is unpredictable.

Above all, it cannot be overemphasized that the creative person is persistent (a fourth P), often to a fault, and patient. The sequence of items in the foregoing list have no priority significance, since different types of creative people will naturally have more or less of certain attributes than others and will assign their own priorities. Different fields demand different strengths, but there are degrees of creativity required in all of them.

Rollo May's *The Courage to Create* (New York: W. W. Norton, 1975) is one of the most high-minded and eloquent treatises on creativity. Here are some of May's richest and most pertinent observations:

"Commitment is healthiest when it is not without doubt, but in spite of doubt." This is historically common to the world's Beethovens, da Vincis, Edisons, Einsteins, Franklins, Shakespeares, Gandhis, Helen Kellers, and Disneys. It can also be made apparent to children.

"Every creative encounter is a new event; every time requires another assertion of courage." This is the driving force and challenge of every performing artist.

"The deeper aspects of awareness are activated to the extent that the person is committed to the encounter." Any musical artist or teacher recognizes that achievement often depends on commitment. This, too, needs to be learned by children. In what more amenable environment could they begin than in the nonthreatening cocoon of the music classroom?

"Reason works better when emotions are engaged." This will come as a surprise to many who think that emotion clouds reason, but those who look for the inspiration of the moment to heighten performance know that May's observation is true.

"Tools and techniques ought to be an extension of consciousness." We have only to contemplate much of today's art, science, and music to see both sides of May's admonition. The same computer technology that can devastate any point on Earth also guides spacecraft to the outer reaches of our solar system and helps us probe cellular structure in search of cures for disease. Synthesized music and images can numb the neurons, but they can also jumpstart children's joy of learning, as on "Sesame Street."

"If it were possible to control the artist—and I do not believe it is—it would mean the death of art." This is exactly what has happened in many totalitarian countries. It can also happen to students under authoritarian teachers anywhere.

"Something is born, comes into being, something that did not exist before—which is as good a definition of creativity as we can get."

"The fact that talent is plentiful but passion is lacking seems to me to be a fundamental facet of the problem of creativity in many fields today, and our ways of approaching creativity by evading the encounter have played directly into this trend. We worship technique—talent—as a way of evading the anxiety of the direct encounter." What more need be said about the difference between a technically fine musician and a great artist?

Overcoming Fears

There are, of course, blocks to creativity, and a knowledge of them is essential, not only for our own creative progress but in order to construct educational experiences for our students. Again, I acknowledge Koberg and Bagnall for articulating these fears, for that is what they are. These include the fear of making mistakes, of being seen as a fool, of being criticized, of being misused, and of being "alone" (a minority of one). We are also afraid of disturbing traditions and making changes, of losing the security of habit, of losing the love of the group, of truly being an individual, and of being wrong. As you can see, it's not easy to be a creative person, but it's reassuring to know that we, as music educators, have the skills, the tools, and the materials to help remove these blocks from the children's roadways by the very nature of the disciplines we practice. We can make a difference in the lives of children.

Be it music, or art,
or theatre, or dance,
Creativity hinges
on taking a chance.

A creative person needs to be aware of the creative process if for no other reason than to avoid being frustrated when success in a project or problem is slow in coming. Research literature essentially agrees that there are four basic phases in the creative process:

1. *Preparation*—getting information and whatever else is necessary to do the job;

2. *Incubation*—letting things develop and hatch in their course; letting the unconscious take over from the conscious;

3. *Illumination*—the eureka or the "aha" moment when all things appear to come together; and

4. *Verification*—when the excitement has passed and only time and testing will tell. Of course, you might find that what you have doesn't work, in which case you return to the preparation period and start all over again. That's how most of the great Broadway musicals were written—trial and error. No song was too sacrosanct to be removed from a show if it didn't work, no matter how much the composer loved it.

Following verification, there is one more phase that I would like to add to the creative process—the "re" factor. This is where the work really begins and perseverance must triumph; it is the heart of the process: The creative person must continually rethink, reconsider, replace, refine, redo, reaffirm, reprocess, rewrite, and reconceptualize. Add your own "re" words to the list. What better lesson could children learn in coping with life than the importance of the "re" component? It is the essence of problem solving, and music lends itself ideally to exploring such "re" opportunities.

If things don't succeed
as envisioned by you,
Rethink, refine,
replace—redo.

The following definition of creativity appears in *The Universal Traveler*. It has depth and poses intellectual challenge. "Creativity can be defined as both the art and the science of thinking and behaving with both subjectivity and objectivity. It is a combination of feeling and knowing; of alternating back and forth between what we sense and what we already know. Becoming more creative involves becoming awake to both; discovering a state of wholeness which differs from the primarily objective or subjective person who typifies our society." The creative person melds these qualities together. You cannot do something unless you know how to do it or can learn how to do it. You can't get excited about something unless some spirit propels you. That feeling of excitement prompts learning and doing, which, in turn, leads to more excitement. Thus, the creative experience is a continuum constantly reinforcing itself.

Becoming Aware

People can become more and more creative by simply becoming more conscious of what it is that they do. The creative person sees the ordinary extraordinarily. Creative adults develop from creative children. Creative people change the world.

For those of us involved in the training of children, understanding the nature of creativity should have high priority. Creative growth, if properly focused, can have an impact on many facets of youngsters' lives. The development of creativity is crucial to the future of our children, our nation, and our world. Education can be instrumental in helping children grow creatively, yet little is done to develop genuine creativity in music and hence in life. A critical component of creative growth is the development of the decision-making process. A child composing a piece of music, be it an environmental sound composition, a song, an accompaniment to a story, or a twelve-tone work, is faced with decision making from beginning to end. That process—being aware of and having to select alternatives—is precisely the type of training that children need as they grow up in an increasingly complex society. They generally do not get it in school, or anywhere else, for that matter.

The music teacher is ideally suited for making children aware of this creative process in music and how it can be carried over to the creative process in other life experiences. Music can encourage some of the attributes common to all creativity, including decision making; overcoming the fear of making mistakes (since mistakes are expected and acceptable); the desirability of individual expression; and the de-emphasis of right and wrong responses, which traditional Western schooling tends to emphasize. Children can begin on their own to search for connections.

The reality of discovery is that more "good" things tend to arise from "mistakes" than correct answers. Had Columbus reached India, America would have waited longer to be "discovered." The discovery of plastics was an accident. If a child is looking for a IV chord and instead finds a chord built on perfect fourths, this mistake might inspire new and even more wonderful sounds. The child should be encouraged to take chances. Right is right, but wrong may be more provocative and vital. The idea that both right and wrong can be creative is one that children can learn through music. We can enjoy both the traditional IV chord and the discovery of perfect fourths.

Being Persistent

Not being afraid to fail is a big educational idea, primary on the list of creative characteristics that children need to develop. What is more frightening than failure? Music training can encourage children to learn from "failures" as well as successes—to fail successfully. An assistant reportedly told Thomas Edison sorrowfully, "We've failed, Mr. Edison, for the 250th time." Edison's reply: "We've not failed. Now we know 250 things that won't work." That type of positive, striving, persistent, open attitude is what music teachers and, indeed, all teachers should want for their students.

> To fail with good purpose
> is a bridge to success.
> Each no is a rung
> on the ladder of yes.

We live in a multidisciplinary, multisensory, multicultural, noncompartmentalized world; our schools are often the opposite. Music teachers can be leaders in reconciling education with the diversity and connections of real life. When children see connections, they see the world more vividly, more meaningfully. We, as music educators, can and should help. With the world crying out for dynamic solutions to ponderous problems, creative children must be our legacy.

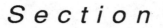

Section

Creativity and the Curriculum

The importance of establishing an organized, systematic approach to creative learning is essential. Both John Kratus and Lyle Davidson provide an understanding of how we can include creativity in the curriculum through the use of clearly articulated goals and objectives.

This may be one of the most important articles on the topic of structuring the music curriculum for active learning because it provides a broad, inclusive, and thorough structural outline. Through the use of objectives, Kratus explains the process needed to ensure the inclusion of creativity in curricular settings.

Structuring the Music Curriculum for Creative Learning

by John Kratus

The role of creativity in the music curriculum is a controversial one that raises many questions. Are creative activities the means by which we educate students? Or are musically creative students the desired ends of our efforts? Does creative functioning in students come only after they have acquired certain basic musical skills and knowledge? Or are creative activities the way we introduce students to these basic skills and knowledge? As a profession, we remain uncertain, and sometimes uncomfortable, about the function of creativity in the music program.

Some have criticized the existing creative approaches to teaching and learning music as being time-consuming and often poorly structured, with ill-defined objectives.[1] According to this position, it is an ineffective use of instructional time to have students simply improvise one ostinato after another or compose endless series of sound compositions with no educational focus. Although music educators have developed a variety of educational activities to stimulate students' creativity, what has largely been lacking is a scheme for bringing structure and sequence to the learning that occurs. For creativity to take its place in the music curriculum, as suggested recently by Bennett Reimer,[2] a set of clearly articu-

John Kratus is an associate professor of music and director of music education at Case Western Reserve University, Cleveland, Ohio. This article appeared in the May 1990 Music Educators Journal.

lated goals and objectives must be developed to guide creative learning. Long-term goals and short-term objectives can be generated using the system described in this article.

Components of Creativity

All instances of organized, complex learning require the teacher to focus the student's development on various components of the process. For example, a guitar teacher is able to break down the complex process of guitar playing by focusing the student's learning in such areas as tone production, left-hand facility, and rhythmic accuracy. In order for this learning to be meaningful, the parts must, of course, be assembled into a whole; in this example, the various learned elements of guitar technique come together as the student progresses, leading to mastery of the instrument. Successful teaching of complex learning requires the teacher to (1) analyze the component parts of the complex behavior, (2) focus the student's development on the components, and (3) enable the student to work toward mastery of the components within the context of the whole.

One difficulty in generating goals and objectives for creative learning is that creative activity seems so complex and varied that the components are hard to discern. Therefore, a necessary first step in curriculum development is to analyze the components that make up creative activity.

Every creative act consists of three components: (1) the person who is creating, (2) the process of creation, and (3) the product that is created. These three components—person, process, and product—can be used as bases in a system for developing goals and objectives. Obviously, these three components are related, but, as in all complex learning, it is useful to focus instruction on various component parts to aid students in attaining mastery of the complex whole.

The person component refers to the personal traits that a creative person brings to a creative act. These traits include originality—the degree to which a person can produce unusual or uncommon responses; fluency—the degree to which a person can produce a number of responses to a problem; and flexibility—the degree to which a person can produce responses that are different from each other. A creative musician is able to bring these personal qualities to bear while composing, improvising, and performing music.

The process component pertains to how creation occurs. Some examples of characteristics of the creative process are problem finding, idea generation, modification of ideas, and evaluation of tentative solutions. Two creative processes in music are improvisation and composition, both of which use these process characteristics. Performers who make decisions about how a particular performance should sound are also engaged in a creative process.

The third component of creativity, the product, is concerned with the result of creative activity. Musical products are the improvisations, compositions, and performances that result when creative musicians engage in creative musical processes. An analysis of musical products could include a description of how musical elements such as form, timbre, the use of tonality, texture, rhythm, meter, and dynamics are used. Another way to characterize a musical product is to consider the use of such musical principles as repetition, development, and contrast.

Goals for Creativity

The three components of creativity suggest three corresponding goals for music education.

(1) The person component suggests the following goal: "students will approach musical activities (improvisation, composition, performance) in a creative manner." This goal underscores the importance of the predisposition or attitude of the student toward engaging in creative activity. Helping students to become more imaginative, more open to solving musical problems, and more musically independent is certainly a worthy educational goal.

(2) A goal derived from the process component is: "students will express themselves musically through improvisation, composition, and creative performance." The focus of this goal is on "how to" engage in these activities. This is an obvious and necessary goal for creative learning, because students must know how to engage in creative musical activities if they are to be musically creative.

(3) The product component of creativity suggests that the teacher look to the musical characteristics of the students' created music: "Students will apply an understanding of musical elements (e.g., rhythm, melody, timbre, dynamics) and musical principles (e.g., repetition, development, contrast) to the production of created music." In working toward this goal, students learn how music works by focusing on musical syntax, or the structure of music, in the context of creative musical activity.

These three long-term goals can serve as guides for creative learning and can be modified to suit the needs of a variety of educational settings and grade levels. Educational goals, however, lack the specificity necessary to guide instruction on a day-to-day basis. Such specificity is possible only through instructional objectives, which can be written to guide students to attain each of the three goals.

Objectives for Creativity

Instructional objectives, as they are usually written, specify the results of learning in terms of predetermined, observable outcomes. For example, the objectives "students will identify by name the sections of the orchestra" and "students will play a C-major scale on the flute" specify predetermined outcomes. Teachers can measure student attainment of the objectives by comparing the students' responses with the predetermined outcomes specified in the objectives.

Creative activities, on the other hand, result in outcomes that cannot be predetermined by the teacher. When a teacher asks a student to compose an ostinato, the teacher does not have in mind a single correct response. Given such unpredictable outcomes, how can a teacher use objectives to structure learning or to determine whether learning has occurred? One way is to use objectives that describe some aspect of the learning encounter or outcome but not the outcome itself. Elliot Eisner referred to these objectives as "expressive objectives."[3]

The behaviors described in an expressive objective for creative activity can be derived from the three components of creativity. In other words, objectives can be classified as person objectives, process objectives, or product objectives, depending on the aspect of the learning encounter or outcome the teacher wishes students to focus on. Student attainment of person, process, and product objectives leads to attainment of the three corresponding goals previously described.

Person Objectives

Person objectives describe musical behaviors that reflect the qualities of creative people. When creative people are given a problem to solve, they are able to come up with unique ideas (originality), many different ideas (fluency), different kinds of ideas (flexibility), fully developed ideas (elaboration) and, in music, ideas that are musically expressive (expressiveness). Each of these qualities can be used by the teacher to formulate person objectives.

Examples of person objectives for originality are: "each student will improvise and repeat a two-measure ostinato different from other students' ostinatos," "small groups of students will invent unusual and unique instruments and compose short sound compositions for them," and "given a short étude, each student will perform it using dynamics unlike those intended by the composer." Some fluency objectives are: "given the first phrase of a song, each student will compose as many second phrases as possible" and "given an assigned piece, each student will phrase the melody in as many ways as possible." A flexibility objective is: "as a group, the class will compose a theme and three variations, with each variation being as different from the others as possible."

Elaboration can be developed using an objective such as: "small groups of students will compose a theme and three variations, with each succeeding variation being more complex than the last." Two objectives designed to develop student expressiveness are: "each student will improvise on the xylophone music to express spring, summer, fall, and winter" and "each student will perform the assigned piece once to express sorrow and once to express joy."

Person objectives can be sequenced in several ways: by steadily increasing the degree to which students must display the qualities in their creative work; by combining two or more person qualities into a single objective; and, in the case of performance activities, by increasing the difficulty of music performed. Another way to sequence person objectives is to vary the level at which creative decisions are made, from the class to small groups to the individual student. Initial creative activities using person objectives can be oriented toward the class as a whole, with the teacher prompting the class with leading questions. Later, creative decisions can be made by students working in small groups and finally by individuals.

Process Objectives

Process objectives describe the nature of the creative activity that students are expected to engage in. Four types of creative activity are (1) exploration, (2) improvisation, (3) composition, and (4) creative performance.

Exploration can be thought of as a precreative activity. Students explore music when they play instruments without truly understanding what sounds will be produced as a result of their actions. Most young children engaged in creative activities with instruments are exploring, because the children do not audiate (hear inwardly with meaning) the sounds they play as they play them. As students continue to explore, they begin to audiate the sounds they are playing, and the musical choices they make while exploring become less random and more intentional. A teacher can help to guide the process first by limiting the musical materials at the student's disposal, then by increasing the available materials. For example, a teacher may limit a student's exploration on a xylophone by removing all but three bars. As the child begins to audiate music produced by the three bars, additional bars can be added. Elements that can be varied in process objectives for exploration are timbre, available pitches, and length of student involvement in the process. An example of a process objective for exploration is: "each student will explore combinations of sounds on a five-bar pentatonic xylophone for two minutes." Exploration objectives can be sequenced by varying the type of timbre and by increasing both the number of pitches that are available to students and length of task involvement.

Improvisation differs from exploration in that a person who is improvising is able to predict the sounds that result from certain actions, whereas a person who is exploring cannot. Improvisations also sound more pattern-dominated than do explorations, because the improviser's ability to audiate what is performed allows him or her to organize the music through the use of repeated patterns. As students become more adept at improvising, they develop strategies for producing and developing musical patterns, and their music becomes less idiosyncratic. Process objectives for improvisation should involve students in becoming progressively better able to structure and control their improvisations. An example of an improvisation objective for beginning students is "while the class sings 'La Bamba,' small groups of students will improvise with hand drums, using rhythm patterns from the song."

Composition activities should follow student involvement with exploration and improvisation. To compose with meaning, students must have the ability to audiate sounds produced on an instrument, which is learned through exploration, and a knowledge of strategies for producing patterns and combinations of sounds, which is learned through improvisation. Unlike improvisation, composition allows the composer time to reflect on the musical ideas produced and to evaluate and modify those ideas. When one is improvising, it is not possible to revise a passage that does not sound quite right, but in composing it is possible to change the final product. It should be noted that improvisation is sometimes referred to as "simultaneous composition," but it is not a type of composition. Instead, composition can be thought of as "reflective improvisation," because time to reflect and change musical ideas is an integral part of the process.

As a student gains greater mastery of the composition process, the ability to generate, modify, and select musical ideas increases. Research suggests that prior to third grade, children with little experience in creating music are able to generate musical ideas, as they do in exploration and improvisation, but they have difficulty in developing and repeating their ideas to produce definitive compositions.[4]

Teachers can help students to improve their compositional skills by showing them how to develop and test musical ideas. This can be accomplished by leading students through group composition activities. As a group composes together, the teacher can ask questions such as "What sounds should come next?" or "Which ending do you prefer?" In effect, through group composition, the teacher can model the process of composition for students. Students can learn to ask themselves similar questions when they compose individually.

Early composition process objectives should focus on those aspects of composition that make it different from improvisation. Specifically, objectives should lead students to modify and evaluate musical ideas. Examples of this kind of objective are: "given a simple melody, each student will think of a way to change the melody slightly" and "given a choice among four phrases, each student will select the phrase he or she likes best and explain why it best fits the first phrase of a two-phrase song." More advanced objectives for composition can specify the degree to which students engage in the composition process, as in the following example: "each student will compose a short theme and then develop the theme at the piano into a longer composition." Composition process objectives can also be sequenced by starting with class compositions, then moving to small-group and individual work.

Creative performance occurs when performers make personal decisions about how a piece should be played. To some extent, every performer is being creative when he or she decides how fast *allegro* is or how loud *forte* should be. Creative performance is similar to the process of composition in that a creative performer thinks of options and then selects the one that sounds most appropriate. Process objectives for creative performance should encourage students to try several ways of playing something and then select the way that sounds best. An example of such an objective is: "each student will perform a piece at three different tempi and select the most appropriate tempo for performance." Beginning creative performance objectives should require students to make performance decisions regarding a single musical element, such as tempo, dynamics, or rubato. As students become more adept at the process of creative performance, several musical elements can be incorporated into a single objective. In addition, it is not necessary to require advanced students to generate multiple options before selecting one, because the generation of possible options becomes automatic. An advanced objective is: "each student will perform a piece using his or her own approach to phrasing and rubato."

Product Objectives

As students improvise, compose, and perform music creatively, their understanding of musical elements and musical organization increases. Another term for musical organization is musical syntax. Meter and tonality are examples of syntax, and when a student composes a song in duple meter, it is an indication that he or she has learned syntax for meter. Evidence from research studies of children's improvisations and compositions implies that children's understanding of musical syntax increases with age, at least until age eleven.[5]

Product objectives describe the musical element or elements to be manipulated while the student creates. Musical elements such as rhythm, meter, tempo, form, phrasing, pitch direction, tonality, harmony, interval size, timbre, texture, dynamics, and articulation can be made the focus of product objectives. Examples of product objectives using musical elements are: "each student will improvise four measures of duple-meter rhythm patterns on the woodblock," "each student will explore timbre pos-

sibilities on a synthesizer," "the class as a whole will compose a sound composition in which the texture changes from monophonic to homophonic to polyphonic," and "given a two-phrase melody, each student will vary the phrases using dynamic changes." Musical principles such as repetition, imitation, development, and contrast can also be used in product objectives. An example of this type of product objective is: "small groups of students will compose a piece that includes imitation between two different timbres."

Product objectives can be sequenced by beginning with instruction for the class as a whole, followed by small-group and individual work. Another way to sequence product objectives is to steadily increase the number of elements or principles in an objective. For example, an advanced objective would be: "each student will compose a song in duple meter, in ABA form, and utilizing development of the music from A in the B section."

Although music educators have developed a variety of educational activities to stimulate student creativity, what has largely been lacking is a scheme for bringing structure and sequence to the learning that occurs.

Product objectives also can be used to complement listening objectives that focus on musical elements and principles. For example, if a listening objective is: "the class will identify entrances of the theme in a fugue," a corresponding creative product objective could be "the class will compose a sound composition in the form of a fugue." Such creative activities help to personalize the learning that occurs in listening lessons and make the learning more meaningful and exciting to students. In addition, person, process, and product objectives can be combined in some cases by developing more than one objective for a single creative activity. It is best, though, not to divide students' attention into too many areas, or the activity will lose its educational focus.

A Word about Evaluation

Most types of educational assessment evaluate the correctness of students' responses. With creative activities, however, no model for correctness exists. This has led some educators to accept all student creations as being equally good. After all, this position argues, if the students put forth a genuine effort, who is to say that one improvisation is better than another? Clearly, this position causes problems, for if a teacher cannot evaluate students' creative work, he or she cannot determine whether learning has occurred.

In assessing students' creative activities, teachers should avoid the trap of evaluating the "goodness" of the created work. Instead, the focus of the evaluation should be on whether students have achieved the behaviors described in the instructional objectives. For example, it should be a relatively simple matter to determine whether a student has performed an étude using original dynamic changes, or whether a small group of students has improvised rhythmic ostinatos to the song "Taffy," or whether the class as a whole has composed a sound composition with three changes in texture. This type of assessment eliminates the need to judge a created work as "good" or "bad," "creative" or "uncreative." Writing specific

goals and objectives can allow for meaningful evaluation of students' creative work and can bring structure and sequence to students' creative music learning.

Notes

1. Charles Leonhard and Robert W. House, *Foundations and Principles of Music Education*, 2nd ed. (New York: McGraw-Hill, 1972), 158, 254-55.

2. Bennett Reimer, "Music Education as Aesthetic Education: Toward the Future," *Music Educators Journal* 75, no. 7 (March 1989): 28-30.

3. Elliot W. Eisner, "Instructional and Expressive Educational Objectives: Their Formulation and Use in Curriculum," in *Instructional Objectives in Music*, ed. J. David Boyle (Reston, VA: Music Educators National Conference, 1974), 39-54.

4. John Kratus, "A Time Analysis of the Compositional Processes Used by Children Ages 7 to 11," *Journal of Research in Music Education* 37, no. 1 (Spring 1989): 5-20.

5. John W. Flohr, "Young Children's Improvisations: Emerging Creative Thought," *The Creative Child and Adult Quarterly* 10, no. 2 (1985): 79-85; John K. Kratus, "Rhythm, Melody, Motive, and Phrase Characteristics of Original Songs by Children Aged Five to Thirteen" (Ph.D. diss., Northwestern University, 1985).

The act of improvisation has long been associated with musicians. In this article, John Kratus looks at the differences between improvisational approaches used by the novice and those used by the expert. In addition to a review of findings in the field, Kratus introduces a multilevel model of how a person becomes an increasingly skilled improviser. Kratus's article is designed to help the educator select an appropriate level of improvisation for students and develop a logical teaching sequence.

Growing with Improvisation

by John Kratus

Try to imagine an improvised duet played by jazz master Lionel Hampton on vibraphone and seven-year-old beginner Sean on an alto xylophone. As the two begin to play, each brings to the task a different set of musical skills and different levels of knowledge and experience. Hampton's fingers fly as he weaves an intricate melodic line over a set of repeating harmonic changes. In the meantime, Sean plays from the lowest note on his instrument to the highest and back again, all the while struggling to keep a steady beat. Are both performers in this example improvising? Or are the differences between the child and the professional so great that comparisons between them are nonsensical?

The answers to these questions have direct implications for how music educators use improvisation in their teaching. Some educators believe that improvisation is a highly sophisticated, technically demanding behavior and should be taught only after a student has developed his or her musicianship and performance skills to an advanced level. Others see improvisation as a natural, intuitive behavior that can be part of preschool music instruction. Depending on one's point of view, instruction in improvisation could begin in preschool or should be delayed until college. A closer look at the nature of improvisation can help determine which position is correct.

John Kratus is an associate professor of music and director of music education at Case Western Reserve University, Cleveland, Ohio. This article appeared in the December 1991 Music Educators Journal.

Actually, beginners and experts share several qualities in their approaches to improvisation. First, all improvisers make purposeful movements to produce sounds in time. The purposeful movements may be coordinated to produce sounds with the body, as when singing or clapping, or with an instrument. Second, all sounds created in improvisation form a part of the final product, and an improviser cannot revise the music after it has been played. In this way improvisation differs from composition, because a composer can take the time to modify, evaluate, and accept or reject musical ideas. The third shared quality is that improvisers have the freedom to choose the pitches and durations while they play, often within certain musical constraints. Some elements such as chord changes, modes, meters, and tempos can be set in advance of an improvisation, but neither the specific sequence of pitches nor their durations are predetermined. In the opening vignette, both Lionel Hampton's improvisation and Sean's shared these qualities.

But to say that all improvisation is the same does not address the vast differences between accomplished improvisers and novices. Clearly, one would not attempt to teach improvisation to a college-level jazz musician and an elementary student in the same way. What is needed is a more precise way of conceptualizing improvisation to allow for changes that occur as students develop knowledge, skills, and experience.

In this article I propose that improvisation can be divided into seven levels of musical behavior. I believe that these levels develop sequentially, and the role of the music educator changes as students move from one level of improvisation to another. This view of improvisation as multileveled is based on the results of research on improvisational behaviors of children and adults and on theoretical models of improvisation.

Studies of Improvisation

A number of researchers have investigated the musical characteristics of young children's improvisations. One of the earliest published studies of children's improvisations was conducted in the 1940s by Gladys Moorhead and Donald Pond at the Pillsbury Foundation School in Santa Barbara, California.[1] Moorhead and Pond observed the improvised chanting and instrumental improvisations of the two- to six-year-olds enrolled in the school. The authors found that with experience the children were able to explore melodic and rhythm patterns in their improvisations. The improvisations that Moorhead and Pond observed were characterized by asymmetrical rhythm patterns, a steady beat, and both simple and compound meters. They also found that when the children first began to improvise on instruments, they focused primarily on exploring timbre and other sound qualities.

John Flohr conducted two studies of young children's improvisations. In his first study, he described the behaviors of four-, six-, and eight-year-old children engaged in improvising on a pentatonic Orff xylophone.[2] Flohr found that the older children's improvisations were more cohesive and had a stronger orientation to a tonal center than did those of the younger children. He also reported that the children he studied were able to improvise patterns and were able to vary their improvisations to convey mood. In his second study, Flohr investigated the musical characteristics of pentatonic xylophone improvisations by children ages two to six years during a four-year period.[3] The results of this second study confirmed that young children can use musical patterns to unify their improvisations.

Based on these results, Flohr proposed three developmental stages in children's improvisation: the *motor energy* stage (ages two to four years), in which the child uses notes of roughly equal duration and repeated pitches; the *experimentation* stage (four to six years), characterized by an emphasis on trying new ideas with little regard for the larger context; and the *formal properties* stage (six to eight years), in which structural characteristics such as tonality and repetition of larger patterns occur.

Deborah Reinhardt examined the rhythmic characteristics of improvisations by 105 three-, four-, and five-year-old children.[4] Reinhardt asked each child to improvise a song on a diatonic alto xylophone while accompanied by a simple bordun played on a bass xylophone. She found that the five-year-olds made greater use of various rhythmic durations and rhythm patterns than the three-year-olds did. Furthermore, almost all the children were able to improvise to the accompaniment with a steady beat and a consistent meter.

The results of the research cited here indicate that young children are capable of improvising music that uses simple structural elements. These findings support the use of improvisational activities as a meaningful part of early-childhood music education. What these studies do not address, however, is the question of what goes on in the mind of the child who is improvising. To use improvisation effectively, teachers should know how students learn to develop and improve their improvisational skills. At present, music education researchers are unable to provide clear descriptions of the underlying cognitive processes that accompany improvisation. The following studies and hypothetical models represent the first attempts to investigate the inner states of improvisers.

An Inside Look

Using an introspective approach, David Sudnow wrote a detailed and fascinating account of his own development as a jazz pianist.[5] He described his learning as occurring in three phases. In the first phase, he developed a vocabulary of patterns or "licks" that he was able to play in a formulative way. The second phase, which he called "going for the sound," was characterized by a more flexible use of patterns together and in variation. In the third phase, "going for the jazz," Sudnow's improvisations became more relaxed, fluid, and coherent.

David Hargreaves and others compared the improvisations of four college students in an introductory jazz improvisation course with improvisations by four expert jazz musicians.[6] After improvising to four backing tracks, subjects were asked what they thought during and after their performances. Results indicated that the college-age novices used one of three strategies while improvising: (1) filling in the time with no organizational plan, (2) emphasizing one musical element (such as rhythm or harmony) in a rather rigid manner, or (3) focusing on one element while remaining open to change as the improvisation progresses. The experts' approach to their improvisations was quite different. All but one expert had some sort of strategy or plan in mind for the improvisation at the outset. These strategies served to organize and unify the improvisation stylistically or through imagery or mood. Furthermore, the experts were able to change their strategies as they improvised; they were relaxed, often used musical clichés, and performed without being conscious of the technical devices they used.

Some educators who have speculated on what goes on in the mind of the improviser have proposed models and offered a number of theories about the process. One such model was developed by Jeff Pressing, who described improvisation as a decision-making process.[7] According to Pressing, an improviser begins with a musical idea or pattern and then extends it using some feature inherent in the pattern. For example, a pattern's rhythm or melodic contour may suggest to the improviser that he or she continue the rhythm or contour in the music that immediately follows. In addition, a good improviser is one who is able to shift attention from one feature to the next while improvising. Among other abilities necessary for good improvisation, Pressing listed the ability to perceive and adjust to relevant changes in the music and the ability to achieve coherence in an improvisation.

P. N. Johnson-Laird developed a model of creativity and applied this model to jazz improvisation.[8] According to the model, the first step in creativity is the generation of ideas or potential solutions to a problem. These initial ideas are evaluated using certain constraints to exclude unreasonable solutions, and among the remaining possible solutions, one is chosen arbitrarily. In jazz improvisation, the constraints involved are the musician's knowledge of musical grammar and the conventions of the musical style being performed. Once a musician knows the stylistic conventions, he or she is able to generate ideas for the direction of the improvisation, determine which of the ideas are acceptable in the style, and then choose almost arbitrarily among the possibilities. Johnson-Laird believes that only the rare innovators are able to break the rules completely and create their own new conventions.

The importance of audiation (hearing music inwardly with meaning) in improvisation was addressed by Edwin Gordon, who wrote, "Unless one can audiate what he is going to create and improvise before he performs it..., all that may be heard at best are the mechanics of scales and arpeggios, and at worst, mere exploration."[9] According to this view, the ability to audiate the patterns that one is improvising is a prerequisite for meaningful improvisation.

Product versus Process

The developmental level and perspective of the improviser should be taken into account when considering the creative musical activity of children and novices. My view is that children and novice improvisers approach the task of improvisation from perspectives quite different from that of an expert improviser.[10] For example, musicians usually think of improvisation as a musical product; that is, music that can be shared with and understood by others. As such, the improviser demonstrates a consciousness of an audience. But this view does not apply to all improvisation and certainly does not apply to much improvisation by young children. Some children create music as a private, exploratory activity, while other children create music to share with others.

When a person creates music for the sake of experiencing the process of creation, that person has a *process* orientation to creativity. When a person creates music that is or could be shared with others, then that person has a *product* orientation. In the duet described earlier, Hampton played music that could be shared with others, because the music was organized according to a series of chord changes that could be followed by the audience. In contrast, Sean probably explored sounds without outside structural references, simply for the sake of engaging in an enjoyable activity.

Another difference between beginners and experts is that an expert is able to match his or her musical intentions with the sounds being performed, whereas a beginner often has difficulty manipulating an instrument or voice effectively enough to match intentions with the sounds produced. Therefore, when listening to a beginner improvise, one should keep in mind that the music produced may not be the same as the music intended by the performer.

To summarize the research and theories on improvisation, young children are capable of rudimentary improvisational behavior, but expert improvisers approach improvisation in a somewhat different way, given the experts' different level of knowledge and skills. To improvise at an expert level, a musician must possess the following:

- The skill to hear musical patterns inwardly as they are about to be played (audiation);
- The knowledge that music is structured in such a way as to allow others to understand it (product orientation);
- The skill to manipulate an instrument or the voice to match the performer's musical intentions fluidly;
- Knowledge of strategies for structuring an improvisation and the flexibility to change strategies, if necessary;
- Knowledge of stylistic conventions for improvising in a given style; and
- The skill to transcend stylistic conventions to develop a personal style.

Seven Improvisation Levels

Given the differences between novice and expert improvisers, it is clear that not all improvisational activity is the same. A more appropriate way to look at improvisation is to conceive of it as being multileveled, consisting of a sequence of different, increasingly sophisticated behaviors. The level at which a student can improvise is determined by the student's level of knowledge and skill. The educational advantage of considering improvisation in this way is twofold: (1) it allows teachers to work with students at a developmentally appropriate level, and (2) it suggests a logical sequence for teaching the knowledge and skills necessary for expert improvisation. The seven levels are as follows:

Level 1: Exploration. Exploration can be thought of as a necessary preimprovisational step. When a student explores on an instrument, he or she tries out different sounds and combinations of sounds in a loosely structured context. The sounds, however, are not guided by audiation, and the improvisation is process-oriented. While exploring, a student begins to discover combinations of sounds that can be repeated. Through the repetition of patterns, students can learn to audiate the patterns, which leads to Level 2. The teacher's role at Level 1 is to provide students with sufficient time to explore and a variety of sound sources for exploration. Exploration activities can be varied by changing timbres (for example, from metallophone to xylophone) or by changing the available pitch materials (such as adding or deleting tone bars). Exploration is a private, creative activity, rather than a group activity.

Level 2: Process-oriented improvisation. Once a student begins to audiate the patterns played in exploration, the resulting music becomes more directed and pattern-dominated. This is Level 2 improvisation, which can be identified by the emergence of cohesive patterns. The student at Level 2 improvises for his or her own pleasure but does not organize the musical material enough through mode or meter to enable others to share the music's meaning. The teacher's role and the educational activities for students improvising at Level 2 are the same as those for Level 1. As the student continues to audiate and use patterns, the student learns to organize the patterns into larger musical structures.

Level 3: Product-oriented improvisation. When a student improvises with a product orientation at Level 3, he or she is conscious of certain external constraints on the music. For example, when a student is able to improvise with a steady pulse, in triple meter, or in a minor tonality, or to the melody of "Jingle Bells," the student shows an awareness of larger structural principles. At this point in the student's development, group improvisation is possible. In implementing activities for Level 3 improvisation, teachers can provide students with different constraints on their improvisations. For example, a teacher may ask students to improvise using a given rhythm pattern or set of chord changes. While improvising at Level 3, students begin to use patterns in a more coherent way, and the performance technique improves.

Level 4: Fluid improvisation. At this level, the student's performance technique is relaxed and fluid. In the case of instrumental improvisation, the student is able to control the instrument so that the technical manipulation of the instrument becomes automatic, and little conscious thought is given to finger placement, embouchure, and similar matters. With vocal improvisation, the voice is equally well controlled. The teacher's role at the fourth level is to focus on the technical facility by providing the student opportunities to improvise in a variety of modes, keys, meters, and tempos. Once the technical problems of improvising are taken care of, the student is better able to concentrate on structuring the improvisation as a whole.

Level 5: Structural improvisation. A student improvising at the fifth level performs with an awareness of the overall structure of the improvisation. The student develops a repertoire of strategies for shaping an improvisation. These strategies may be nonmusical (such as moods or images) or musical (such as modes or development of patterns). The teacher's role is to suggest or model different means for giving structure to an improvisation. As a student develops proficiency in structuring an improvisation, he or she begins to shift strategies while improvising. At this point, the student is ready to improvise stylistically.

Level 6: Stylistic improvisation. A Level 6 improvisation is one in which the student improvises skillfully within a given style. The student learns various melodic, harmonic, and rhythmic characteristics of a style and gains skill in incorporating those characteristics into an improvisation. A teacher can demonstrate for the student what the conventions and clichés of a style are. Recordings can also be used

effectively to model a style. For a time, students who are learning to achieve Level 6 may benefit from direct imitation of models. For most musicians, education in improvisation ends at Level 6. Only the most proficient improvisers can advance to the highest level of improvisation.

Level 7: Personal improvisation. The seventh level is achieved by those musicians who are able to transcend recognized improvisation styles to develop a new style. Miles Davis is an example of this kind of musician. To a certain extent, all improvisation is personal, but Level 7 improvisation breaks new ground and establishes its own set of rules and conventions. Oddity or originality for its own sake does not produce a Level 7 improvisation. To help a student develop to the seventh level, a teacher can be encouraging and supportive of experimentation. But the teacher cannot have expectations for what a Level 7 improvisation might sound like, because there would be no way to predict what the new style would be.

Sequencing Instruction

To help students develop their improvisational skills, music educators can provide structured opportunities for students to improvise at the appropriate level and assist them in advancing from one level to the next. In a recent article for *MEJ*, I suggested an approach for writing and sequencing objectives for creative music activities.[11] The method described in that article could be used to generate objectives at any of the seven levels of improvisation.

There are two rules to keep in mind when using the levels to sequence instruction in improvisation. First, advancing from one level to the next requires attainment of the knowledge and skills of the preceding level. The knowledge and skills that students develop at a certain level, however, need not be taught only at that level. For example, while a student is working at Level 3 (product-oriented improvisation), the teacher could introduce some characteristics of specific improvisational styles, which would be the primary educational focus of Level 6 (stylistic improvisation). The teacher should not expect, though, that the student at Level 3 would be able to meaningfully incorporate those stylistic characteristics in an improvisation.

The second rule for using the levels in teaching improvisation is this: students cannot skip levels as they advance to higher levels, but they may revert to lower levels for a variety of reasons. For example, if the tempo increases too much or if an asymmetrical meter is used, a student can revert from Level 5 (structural improvisation) to Level 3 (product-oriented improvisation) until he or she is able to play fluidly. If a student at Level 6 (stylistic improvisation) encounters a new style, there can be a similar reversion. The instrument on which the performer improvises can affect the level of improvisation, as in the case of the student who improvises at a high level on saxophone and on a lower level on piano. The performer's mood also determines the level of improvisation, as when as expert capable of improvising at Level 7 (personal improvisation) chooses to "doodle" privately at Level 2 (process-oriented improvisation). Therefore, a student may revert from a higher level to a lower level when encountering a difficult musical element, a new musical style, or a change in mood.

A Chance to Grow Musically

To understand how the levels of improvisation can be used to sequence instruction, consider the example of Jamie learning to improvise on clarinet. Jamie's first efforts at creating music (Level 1) sound like a discordant jumble. Jamie tries various combinations of fingerings on the clarinet and explores the sounds that result. Jamie's teacher suggests that Jamie spend a few minutes every day exploring different combinations of the pitches that have been learned. Gradually Jamie is able to hear the sounds inwardly as they are produced, and the exploration gives way to music that has some discernable patterns but no overall cohesiveness (Level 2). The teacher still recommends that Jamie spend a few

---

Developmental Levels of Improvisation

Level 1. The student tries out different sounds and combinations of sounds in a loosely structured context.

Level 2: *Process-oriented improvisation.* The student produces more cohesive patterns.

Level 3: *Product-oriented improvisation.* The student becomes conscious of structural principles such as tonality and rhythm.

Level 4: *Fluid improvisation.* The student manipulates his or her instrument or voice in a more automatic, relaxed manner.

Level 5: *Structural improvisation.* The student is aware of the overall structure of the improvisation and develops a repertoire of musical or nonmusical strategies for shaping an improvisation.

Level 6: *Stylistic improvisation.* The student improvises skillfully within a given style, incorporating its melodic, harmonic, and rhythmic characteristics.

Level 7: *Personal improvisation.* The musician is able to transcend recognized improvisation styles to develop a new style.

minutes every day freely improvising, and the teacher points out the patterns in Jamie's improvisations.

As the patterns in Jamie's improvisations become more pervasive, and as Jamie begins to develop a sense of meter and tonality, the teacher begins to place certain constraints on the improvisations (Level 3). The teacher may clap a pulse and direct Jamie to improvise at that tempo. As Jamie develops a greater understanding of meter, tonality, and harmony, the teacher may ask her to play an improvisation in duple meter and in C major, using the chords I-IV-I-V-I. After a while, Jamie's technical understanding of meter, tonality, and harmony improves to the extent that she is able to devote greater concentration to developing increased facility on the clarinet while improvising (Level 4). Jamie's teacher encourages this development by providing her with opportunities to improvise solo and in small groups while playing in different modes, keys, meters, and tempos.

Jamie's music at this point sounds a little stiff, as if the performer were "going through the motions." To break through this stiffness, the teacher asks Jamie to structure improvisations in ways that transcend simple obedience to the rules of meter and tonality (Level 5). For example, Jamie is asked to improvise "moody music that gradually becomes brighter," and "music that becomes increasingly dissonant." The teacher may also have Jamie analyze recordings of improvised solos to study how other musicians structure their improvisations. At this point, Jamie is ready to focus on improvising within certain established styles (Level 6). Jamie's teacher demonstrates some of the characteristic "licks" and playing techniques in a style, such as Dixieland, cool jazz, or hard bop. The teacher also asks Jamie to study and imitate recordings of various performers such as Benny Goodman and Pete Fountain. Only if Jamie is a truly outstanding improviser will a completely new, individual style emerge (Level 7). To help Jamie reach this level, the teacher could push her to break through the boundaries and conventions of established styles.

This model of developmental levels of improvisation offers an approach for using improvisation throughout a child's education. Improvisation is not simply an intuitive musical behavior, nor is it only an activity reserved for the most proficient musi-cians. It is both, and improvisation can and should be a meaningful part of every student's music education, from preschool through adulthood.

Notes

1. Gladys Moorhead and Donald Pond, *Music for Young Children* (Santa Barbara, CA: Pillsbury Foundation for the Advancement of the Arts, 1978, originally published 1941-51).

2. John Warren Flohr, "Musical Improvisation Behavior of Young Children" (Ph.D. diss., University of Illinois at Urbana-Champaign, 1979).

3. John Flohr, "Young Children's Improvisations: Emerging Creative Thought" *Creative Child and Adult Quarterly* 10 (1985): 79-85.

4. Deborah A. Reinhardt, "Preschool Children's Use of Rhythm in Improvisation" *Contributions to Music Education* 17 (Fall 1990): 7-19.

5. David Sudnow, *Ways of the Hand: The Organization of Improvised Conduct* (Cambridge: Harvard University Press, 1978).

6. David J. Hargreaves, Conrad A. Cork, and Tina Setton, "Cognitive Strategies in Jazz Improvisation: An Exploratory Study" (Paper delivered at the International Society for Music Education Research Symposium, Stockholm, Sweden, August 1990).

7. P. N. Johnson-Laird, "Reasoning, Imagining, and Creating," *Bulletin of the Council for Research in Music Education*, no. 95 (Winter 1987): 71-87.

8. Jeff Pressing, "Improvisation: Methods and Models," in *Generative Processes in Music*, ed. John A. Sloboda (Oxford, England: Oxford University Press, 1988).

9. Edwin E. Gordon, "Audiation, Music Learning Theory, Music Aptitude, and Creativity," *Proceedings of the Suncoast Music Education Forum on Creativity*, ed. John W. Richmond (Tampa, FL: University of South Florida, 1989), 78.

10. John Kratus, "Orientation and Intentionality as Components of Creative Musical Activity," in

Proceedings of the Suncoast Music Education Forum on Creativity, ed. John W. Richmond (Tampa, FL: University of South Florida, 1989).

11. John Kratus, "Structuring the Music Curriculum for Creative Learning," *Music Educators Journal* 76, no. 9 (May 1990): 33–37.

Lyle Davidson discusses the importance of addressing creativity in the context of a collaborative music assessment environment such as the one established in the Arts Propel project. Davidson explains how individual creativity can be enhanced by using specific instructional equipment such as computers and instruments, through performance, and via composition.

Tools and Environments for Musical Creativity

by Lyle Davidson

When considering assessment, one does not think immediately of creativity. However, in Arts Propel, a collaborative music assessment project taking place in Pittsburgh, creativity is one of the issues that leaps out. Students constantly bring up issues of creativity in interviews that take place throughout the year.

Sponsored by the Rockefeller Foundation, Arts Propel brings together the Pittsburgh Public Schools, Educational Testing Service, and Harvard Project Zero to develop ways of assessing students' musical knowledge more comprehensively. The comments and examples in this article come from two composition projects, illustrating contexts within which creative thought and practice can be fostered. The first project, "Songsmith," piloted in Boston schools, is being used in a variety of classes in Pittsburgh where melody writing and text setting are taught to beginning students who have little or no musical background. It requires the use of the program *Deluxe Music Construction Set* (published by Electronic Arts) and Macintosh computers to set students' limericks to music. The second composition domain project, "First Melody," is part of an eighth-

Lyle Davidson is a lecturer in education at Harvard University's Graduate School of Education and chair of the Undergraduate Theory Department at the New England Conservatory of Music. This article originally appeared in the May 1990 Music Educators Journal.

grade general music class in which students learn how to compose and perform antecedent and consequent phrases, playing their compositions on bell sets.

This article is based on interviews that occur during specific instructional frameworks called domain projects. There are domain projects for private lessons, ensembles, and general music classes. Every domain project includes three essential ingredients of learning in the arts: production, reflection, and perception. Production is the starting point of all domain projects. It requires activity, whether making music as a performer or a composer or sketching the path of one's perceptions while listening to a piece. Production is the best means for engaging the musical impulse, and it becomes an occasion for reflection.

Reflection, no doubt, can occur as aesthetic contemplation. But in Arts Propel, reflection is linked to the activity of performing, making, or notating music. It is intimately connected with the process of monitoring and shaping a performance, a composition, or a notation. It mirrors the thinking involved in planning, designing strategies, making choices, and evaluating results, as well as quietly enjoying a completed work.

Without perception, production and reflection are moot. Perception refers to the powers of discrimination on which both production and reflection depend. In an Arts Propel domain project, production, reflection, and perception are present in a flexible and fluid relationship to one another, so that students can exercise and integrate all three as they see fit, rather than through a sequence of rigid work units examining each trait in isolation from the others. While domain projects are not described to students in these terms, students refer to production, reflection, and perception indirectly in their journals and interviews. They understand that writing a melody requires listening and looking for patterns and relationships and thinking about the effect on the composition:

> I like to correct the notes. It's fun. It makes you use your ear, your eye, your brain. Sometimes you get mad because it takes a lot of time, but there is something in the song you don't feel right. It takes time. Just be patient.

This student, Thad, suggests that considerable reflection is necessary in order to discover what might and might not be a satisfactory idea, how to work out the implications of the best idea, and what is required to produce a satisfactory result. Furthermore, he understands that he is responsible for shaping his melody toward the idea he wants it to convey. During his early attempts at planning what he will do for his text-setting project, Thad said,

> This part is the fun part, but hard, too. I have to decide whether I want my limerick to be strong or weak or whatever. Then I can express that on my melodies. Well, I want my melody to be strong and full of hopes. How am I going to do that? I just use those notes and this rhythm. Like I said before, it is kind of hard to make up the melodies for your song.

Three important factors bearing on creativity have emerged during our work in assessment: (1) the empowerment of students made possible by using computers, (2) the importance of conducting classes in the language of music—sound, and (3) the importance of characteristics common to the music classroom but less often found in other classrooms.

Computers and Music

Using a computer as a compositional tool forces a reconsideration of basic musical skills. It raises perhaps unsettling but important questions about the relationship of musical knowledge to the traditional skills of music reading and performance. Although learning music notation traditionally requires many years of practice, a computer makes music notation immediately

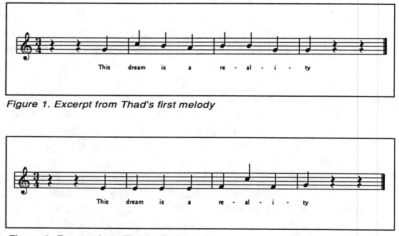

Figure 1. Excerpt from Thad's first melody

Figure 2. Excerpt from Thad's first revision

available for composition. The first example shows the first draft of a melody created by Thad using "Songsmith." In spite of having had no previous experience with music or computers, Thad began shaping this melody after a very short period of instruction (see figure 1).

What performance ability is necessary to realize the sounds of this notated sketch? Thad needs only to execute two keystrokes in sequence to hear what he has written. Years of instruction have shrunk to a single sequence of gestures. The computer does not make learning an instrument undesirable, however. Since the computer only plays back the stark notation, bare of nuance, an instrument is still necessary to interpret it musically.

But the computer is more than a tool with which to represent musical knowledge. With it, students can discover important musical relationships for themselves:

> I was so surprised that there is a relationship between the first note and the last note of the song. They are on the same rhythm and sometimes are the same notes. I have never noticed this before.

Thus, the computer becomes a tool for exploration, verification, and confirmation.

Language of Instruction
Performance, whether on computers or on simple instruments like bell sets, provides an additional language for music classes: the sound of pitches and rhythms. This accomplishes three very important things: It links concepts expressed in words to sound, it expands students' reference base by bringing the music literature they know together with the musical images of the ideas they are trying to create, and it makes revision a more immediate part of the compositional process.

Musical concepts, terms, and definitions are often taught verbally rather than through composition and performance. Because of the premium put on verbal and written language as the medium of instruction in schools, the connection between musical concepts and musical expression is not necessarily clear. Students memorize musical terms and their definitions as though they were to be used in conversation or on pencil-and-paper examinations, not for music making or critical listening.

Hearing a version or a sketch of a melody played not only links concepts to sound, it also expands on verbal descriptions of ideas by bringing another modality of knowledge—sound—into the compositional process. When students hear one version of a piece, they can compare it with the music they already know or are trying to express. Hearing the sound of a piece greatly changes the reference system in which choices and judgments are made. Drawing on their aural knowledge, students can evaluate their work on the basis of a fuller representation, and, if necessary, can revise it to better match the melody they have in mind. As Thad describes:

> I just finished two more melodies. I like both a lot, but still I'm a little not quite sure of what I want. I want it to be strong, but some points are still quite weak. So I need to work more on it.

Doodles, sketches, and drafts provide clues about the cognitive processes that underlie the effort of shaping ideas. Making choices, evaluating them, and shaping them are central activities in the arts. From this perspective, revisions are the footprints of thought.

In conventional classes, revision is not often an integral part of the learning process. Students make few revisions; most prefer to make no changes at all. But wherever students are engaged, they have little difficulty working a problem over and over to get the effect they want. Their effort, so willingly undertaken when their level of personal commitment is high, is captured by Thad:

> Miss Van Dyne asked me some questions about my works. I showed her my newest melody for my limerick. She said it is great, but I didn't really like that melody that much. I have to work on it a little bit more.
> [Still later] Working and working. Finally I got what I want. This is it. [See figure 2.]

Performance, whether on the computer or a simple instrument, has a profound effect on the place of revision in the writing process. When a computer is available, no one can resist the playback feature. Students, beginning and experienced alike, write a few notes and press "play" to hear what they wrote. Liz describes the effect of playing a version of her melody on a set of bells during the "First Melody" project:

> I like to criticize the songs. If one note stands out, that's it. You can tell. If I hear one note that sounds really bad, I say "stop right there" and go right back and change it.

Students who write and perform melodies begin to learn what it feels like to be a Johann Sebastian Bach, a Ludwig van Beethoven, or a Burt Bacharach. Simple instruments effectively enable them to bring notation and performance together with sufficient clarity for them to understand the connection between composition and performance.

Classroom Values

Computers and instruments can be powerful tools for creating music. But creative work will not occur without a supportive environment. Our work in Pittsburgh suggests that the classroom that supports creative work may have to subscribe to very different values from those that govern the classroom where traditional academic subjects are taught. Although these conditions may be difficult to achieve within a given school environment, classes should be designed to (1) allow extended periods of time to work on basic problems and projects, (2) allow flexible schedules in order to match the individual working styles of students, (3) provide open-ended learning situations so that students can bring their entire musical experience to bear on the tasks, (4) allow students to define and frame problems for themselves, (5) develop judgment and critical abilities, not merely accuracy, and (6) involve students by engaging them in real-life tasks and giving them more responsibility for undertaking their own learning.

1. Long-term engagement with significant problems. Music classes provide a model of education where learning takes place over long periods of time. Continued lessons, rehearsals, and projects that extend over longer periods of time change the scope of the learning activity. Students have the opportunity to see evolution of their ideas. While learning to compose melodies or to perform pieces, students have time to make many opportunities for reflection on objectives, strategies, and outcomes of the problem.

As students begin to learn about a problem, their relationship to it changes. Ultimately, their perspective on the nature of the task, the definition of the objective, the strategies employed to reach the goal, and the criteria for evaluating the result all change. What appeared to be the problem at the outset shifts with experience. For example, a student may be most concerned about the

rhythm of a melody at first. Later, after some experience, the pitches may become a more important factor.

Working over an extended period of time, students begin to develop an understanding of the breadth of a problem or topic. They have many opportunities to relate different levels of criteria and solutions from their personal experience while at the same time drawing on a broader frame of reference, integrating the range of their experience from both inside and outside school.

Thad comments on the effect of the new rhythmic feature Miss Van Dyne introduces, replacing even quarter notes with notes of longer and shorter durations:

> Well, this is some hard. First the limerick, then melodies, and now this. It's kind of hard to put the right kind of note for each word. If you make one little mistake the song will sound ridiculous.

2. Self-paced work. Students appreciate the flexibility of the music class and prize the teacher who can entrust students with the responsibility for their own projects. The following response is commonly heard in interviews:

> Music class is important because you don't have to work under pressure. [The teacher] lets you do it another time, like during lunch or homeroom.

This flexibility has important repercussions for students. For example, in a music class where creative thinking is the focal point, the object is to allow students to generate the best solutions of which they are capable. Also, while some students work quickly, others require more time to achieve the results they are seeking. Thus, individual students can complete assignments according to their own capacity and pace. Students can approach and leave their work in a far less regimented way than occurs in most classes.

Ideally, students should be able to leave if work is not going well, whether because of a block or because the feeling is not just right, as this student observes:

> I was not feeling so well. In this kind of situation, I couldn't put my mind on anything. So I just left it like that. Late that afternoon I came down here again and chose Miss Van Dyne's solution.

Alternatively, students should be able to work ahead on their projects if they are having a productive day.

> I finished my limerick, so I just made up a song on the computer for fun.

Finally, schools provide surprisingly few opportunities for students to accomplish their best work. The demands of schedule and routine play too important a role. By creating situations in which students can work when they are most productive, the school ensures that students will gain the satisfaction of knowing they have done their best work.

3. Open-ended learning situations. Students bring resources to class that extend beyond the classroom walls. Interviews with students reveal that a great many are regularly involved in composing and arranging as well as performing outside of school. All the students say they listen to music during most of their waking hours. Many report that they go to sleep listening to their favorite tape or radio station. They say that this repertory provides models for their melodic compositions.

Educators want to know the extent to which lessons learned in one context transfer to other contexts. Concepts learned in writing melodies can transfer to other musical contexts, as the comments of a seventh-grade student currently working on the "First Melody" domain project make clear. She is explaining how she thinks popular singer Debbie Gibson wrote her songs:

> They're full of patterns. Just like the melodies we compose in class. They have parts that go up [antecedent phrases] and then parts that go down [consequent phrases].

She is also beginning to understand from firsthand experience what makes melodies co-herent. When discussing the songs of a current popular singer, she points out that his melodies that "keep the notes close together" (i.e., use stepwise motion) sound better than those that do not.

Another student reports that in addition to the ideas she got for her melodies outside of school, it was important to hear the work of her peers:

> I think it's important to compare your work with other kids, because I learned different rhythms from them.

Finally, an open environment allows students to draw on the advice of others. In spite of the clearly collaborative and social nature of every adult's work habits, schools are structured as though the only worthwhile work is done independently. A student using "Songsmith" commented on the value of being able to get advice from his friends, a resource from outside his class:

> I also finished my duet by the help of my friends. They listened to it and gave me some suggestions. So I took their suggestions and tried to correct it.

4. Problems defined and framed by the student. Music classes provide contexts for creative and independent thinking. Problems are typically presented in "grown-up" fashion, with all the ambiguities present—each ambiguity a ready lure for the unsuspecting novice, who must exercise judgment and skill while wrestling with the same problems as those facing the expert practitioner.

Students appreciate the chance to address such rich problems. For example, in spite of the fact that all the students use the same pitches, meter and rhythmic durations, and formal structure when completing their assignments in the "First Melody" project, one student volunteers:

> The best thing about my class is that I can work on my own. The way Miss Green teaches it, we do our own work and we do it on our own.

Students interviewed report that music teachers, unlike teachers of other subjects, do not demonstrate what to do or give out solutions to problems unless the student needs help. Students are engaged by the opportunity to form and solve their own problems.

Students also value the specialness of their music class. In other classes, they are all expected to reach the same solution for a given problem. In music class, students are expected to come up with results that may be quite different. And, in music class, unlike other classes—where attention, seriousness, and effort typically pay off with accurate solutions, correct answers, and correspondingly high grades— the best work is not necessarily that of the best behaved, most serious student. Carol spoke about another student's work during her interview about the "First Melody" domain project:

> David was the best in class. But I don't see how he does it.... I guess you could say he is the class clown. I don't know how Miss Green puts up with him. She sent him to the office once. But some of his melodies—even the ones he just played around with—were really good.

In the context of a creative class, students discover their own problems and, therefore, invent their own solutions. This means that there must be a variety of successful answers. These answers may change as the student's perspective on the issues changes. During one of his attempts to write a limerick, Thad said:

> I like music and I like limericks, too. It sounded fun. But when writing by yourself with the topic "The American Dream," it's kind of hard. It's easy for me to do it in a free way. By (doing it) my way, I have the first line of the limerick. I am working on the second now.

Later, he talked about changes he needs to make:

> Have to name my limerick. How about "The American Dream Is Reality"? No, too common.

"Reality and You." This sounds nice. I got the name and my favorite melody. I'm ready to turn it in for Miss Van Dyne's opinion.

5. Development of judgment. In academic classes, the "expert" is the model. The expert values accurate and comprehensive recall and argument from evidence according to logical constructs and principles. Eighty-percent levels of accuracy are often sufficient.

In music classes, however, the model is the creative artist. In music, the values include construction of a convincingly expressive moment, the exercise of judgment that is sensitive to the nuance of the context, and the ability to create integrity persuasively across a whole shape by constructing a network of relationships from the elements of music.

Because the required level of accuracy in music is necessarily so high, critical evaluation and choice play a more important role in the educational exchange. Just how much to exaggerate dynamics or articulations, when and by how much to slow down, and whether a melody needs more stepwise motion are not issues of accuracy but of judgment. Significantly, these standards apply to all the students engaged in music, the gifted and the less-than-gifted alike.

The process of revision plays an important role in the development of judgment. By being confronted constantly with the results of past choices, a student must constantly re-evaluate the nature of the problem and the appropriateness of the solution.

> Finally, at the end of class, I had finished. I think this is my final one to give to Miss Van Dyne. But I am not sure. I may come up with a better one tomorrow. Then, maybe I will change my mind.
>
> I had finished two more (songs). I seem to like the last one the best. It is the right one for my limerick. I had to try to find the right one for my limerick, but it came out not right. This time it is the perfect one. I will change the melody for added rhythmic interest. (See figure 3).

Figure 3. Excerpt from Thad's second revision

6. *Student empowerment.* Lisa, a student in Miss Green's "First Melody" class, says she is getting a sense of what a composer does:

> You get to know the pitches in your head. You get to know how it sounds before you put in down on paper, because we sing "do, re, mi, fa, sol" before we begin.

Thad's summary of his experience is somewhat different:

> Like I said before, it's kind of hard to make up the melodies for your song. With patience and time you will finish it. A composer. You are the hero, a star. That is what it's like to be a composer. You have done something great for yourself, make songs for people to hear.

Thad neither reads music notation nor plays an instrument, but the computer and the materials of "Songsmith" made it possible for him to learn something about being a librettist and a composer. And the pride Thad takes in his composition is clear. He is proud that he successfully defined and solved a problem in which he had considerable personal investment. The class in melody writing and text setting provided a context within which he could understand what it means to locate problems that are meaningful to him, use his judgment and skills to solve his problems according to his own criteria, do something well, exercise his own taste, and finally, share the results of his work with others. There is no question but that Thad has learned important lessons about music and added an important positive dimension to his sense of self as a result of this class.

General music classes are probably not the training ground for performers or composers, but they are the first arenas in which students, regardless of gift, can discover what thinking like an artist means and how creative thinking transforms expectations, standards, and conditions of learning. And students begin to understand what the rewards of an artist's work might be. In music classes, where the conditions for creativity prevail, students get to face themselves and wrestle with the opportunities and excitement that result from every encounter with creativity.

Suggested Readings

Davidson, Lyle, and Larry Scripp. "Education and Development in Music from a Cognitive Perspective." In *Children and the Arts*, edited by David J. Hargreaves, 59–86. Bristol, PA: Open University Press, 1989.

Davidson, Lyle, and Larry Scripp. "Tracing Reflective Thinking in the Performance Ensemble." *The Quarterly* [now *The Quarterly Journal of Music Teaching and Learning*], 1, nos. 1–2 (Double issue), 49–62.

Davidson, Lyle, and Larry Scripp. "Young Children's Musical Representations: Windows on Music Cognition." In *Generative Processes in Music*, edited by John Sloboda, 195–230. Oxford: Oxford University Press, 1988.

Davidson, Lyle, Larry Scripp, and Patricia Welsh. "'Happy Birthday': Evidence for Conflicts of Perceptual Knowledge and Conceptual Understanding." *Journal for Aesthetic Education* 22, no. 1 (Spring 1988): 65–74.

Gardner, Howard. "On Assessment in the Arts: A Conversation with Howard Gardner." *Educational Leadership* 45 (December 1987/January 1988): 30–34.

Gardner, Howard. "Zero-Based Arts Education: An Introduction to Arts Propel." *Studies in Art Education* 30, No. 2 (September 1989): 71–83.

Scripp, Larry, Joan Meyaard, and Lyle Davidson. "Discerning Musical Development." *Journal for Aesthetic Education* 22, no. 1 (Spring 1988): 75–88.

Wolf, Dennie. "Portfolio Assessment: Sampling Student Work." *Educational Leadership* 46 (April 1989): 35–39.

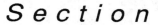

Section

Incorporating Creativity in the Classroom

The importance of incorporating creativity in the classroom through the use of action studies and ideas cannot be underestimated. If philosophical, definitional, and curricular implementation discussions are important, then the means of finding ways to begin the creative process must be of equal or greater importance.

In section 3, in John Kratus's article "Structuring the Music Curriculum for Creative Learning," it was suggested that curricular offerings include creative activities based on exploration, improvisation, composition, and creative performance. The articles in this section offer "how to" ideas in one or more of the creative activities suggested by Kratus.

In this article, Hollis Thoms presents ideas for developing musical imagination or creativity at the secondary level through the use of musical compositions. He also discusses the decision-making process in relation to creativity and aesthetics.

Encouraging the Musical Imagination through Composition

by Hollis Thoms

n *A Little Schubert* by M. B. Goffstein, Franz Schubert, drawn affectionately with curly hair and large, round glasses, lives in a sparsely furnished, unheated room where he sits at a small table and writes music. He hears music when his friends hear nothing and he hears more music than he can possibly write down.

The Musical Imagination

Roger Sessions wrote that "a composer's mind is constantly ready for the activity of composition,"[1] and John Cage said the same thing in a different way when he wrote that "there is no such thing as silence. Something is always happening that makes a sound."[2] In order to compose music one must hear sounds; one must be able to attend to the sounds of the outside and inside soundscapes. To be a composer means being ready to transform experience into significant sound images. It also means that one has such a driving desire and compelling need to manipulate sounds that it becomes an obsession.

Hollis Thoms is a composer, educator, and communications consultant in River Forest, Illinois. This article originally appeared in the January 1987 Music Educators Journal.

Students don't know that such attending, readiness, and desire exist unless they are given the opportunity to explore, develop, and arouse these states in a continuous and consistent manner. Music classes should give students such opportunities. On the elementary school level, a number of compositional activities have provided such opportunities for students. These include improvising narrative works using Orff instruments, improvising with a variety of instruments using an electronic piece as a catalyst, setting poems to music, creating a piece based on a simple harmonic progression, and collecting sounds from the environment and manipulating them on tape.

Most of the compositional experiences are accomplished with very little abstract reflection. The experiences are spontaneous and fresh. The purpose of these compositional activities is to provide students with an opportunity to develop an awareness that such activities are indeed possible and part of music making. For example, studying the violin doesn't just mean learning the correct hand position or memorizing a piece for a recital. It also means using one's skill on the instrument to explore both the sounds of the violin and one's musical imagination at the same time.

Going One Step Farther

On the high school level, students go a step farther and begin to "think" about their compositional attending, readiness, and desires. Three projects have worked particularly well in helping students think as composers. The first is the development of a set of variations based on the very familiar tune "Ah, vous dirai-je, maman" (composer uses pre-existing musical material to generate musical ideas). The second is a theater piece based on a children's book by Maurice Sendak called *Where the Wild Things Are* (composer uses literary work to generate musical ideas). The third is an interdisciplinary visual art, dance, and music experience focusing on the concept of line in those arts (composer uses other arts and an abstract concept to generate musical ideas).

The first project resulted from listening to Wolfgang Amadeus Mozart's *Twelve Variations on "Ah, vous dirai-je, maman,"* K.265. We listened to the set of variations and followed the line of musical thought that Mozart was developing as he worked with the simple theme. The students were to come to some conclusions about what and why Mozart did what he did to the theme and what the overall effect was. We talked about how he manipulated the theme, increased or decreased the intensity, changed the mood through sudden shifts of tempo, key or texture, and how each of the three was embellished or merely suggested in each variation.

After listening to the piece each student:

1. took the "Ah, vous dirai-je, maman" theme and composed a variation in either the key of F major/minor or C major/minor;

2. played the variation on the recorder;

3. wrote out the variation that had been composed (this included work on calligraphy and notation);

4. played everyone's variation; and

5. designed a set using all the variations with an accompanying written essay explaining how the aesthetic decisions were made (this was the most important aspect of the assignment).

For the last part of the assignment, the students were given a "test," after they had thought about their set of variations. They were asked to place them where they wanted it played (at the beginning, end, middle, or beginning and end), and then, in the boxes provided, they inserted the initials of each student's name (referring to the variation) in the

order they had chosen. Second, they had to write in *one* sentence how they had organized the set of variations. We talked about the various possibilities, such as going from the simplest to the most complex (and vice versa); going from the closest to the theme to the most distant from the theme; going from the slowest to the fastest; going through a sort of arch form; increasing tension through the insertion of significant pauses and changes of pace; and alternating major and minor or various time signatures.

Wrestling with Decisions

When confronted with a conventional, musical composition problem such as how to create a set of variations on a given theme students were encouraged to "think" as composers and wrestle with aesthetic decisions. In this way, they had to develop a line of musical thought. The students began to think of composing as more than just making interesting sounds; it also involved making decisions about the sequence and placement of those sounds in the design of an entire work.

Because composers often cull musical ideas from literary works, the second project was a musical setting generated by Sendak's *Where the Wild Things Are*. In preparation for this assignment, students listened to three works that used literary works in completely different ways: Claude Debussy's *Prelude à l'apres-midi d'un faune*, based on a poem by Stephane Mallarmé; Joseph Schwantner's recent *New Morning for the World*, based on the words of Martin Luther King, Jr.; and John Harbison's *Full Moon in March*, based on a strange text by William Butler Yeats. Students worked in groups of three of four, used the piano and Orff instruments, and were allowed to use the Sendak text in any way they wanted. They could:

1. compose a purely musical rendition suggesting the narration of the text (like the Debussy), or

2. compose music to accompany a spoken narration of the text (like the Schwantner), or

3. compose an opera-like adaptation of the narration (like the Haribson).

The students submitted works in all three categories, but the ones that were the most successful were of the second type. One group incorporated an arch form design into the overall musical material (ABCBA) as well as a I-V-I harmonic design. In the A section, Max is mischievous and his mother sends him to his room. To suggest the little boy's mischief, the students used the tonic. While in his room, Max's imagination begins to take over and the forest begins to grow in his room. To mirror this, the group built up a series of ascending thirds on the alto glockenspiel and alto metallophone. In the B section, Max goes off in a private boat over an ocean to where the wild things are. The group created floating sounds here to mimic the action. In the C section, Max is where the wild things are and makes a tremendous rumpus.

At this point the group tried some experimental sounds inside the piano, clusters on the keyboard, and percussion. By this time, they appropriately had modulated to the dominant because Max was the farthest from "home" at this point. After the rumpus, Max gets into his boat and goes over the ocean (once again the B section) to his room (the A section) where there is no longer any forest (the group played an inversion of the forest material) and back to some hot supper his mother had left for him.

Thinking Like a Composer

Transforming a literary work into musical ideas is another typical composer "problem" that requires students to think like composers. The process composers use to compose onto a literary work is mysteriously intuitive but very real. Somehow sounds take shape from words. *Where the Wild Things Are* is a simple yet evocative book that helps students create musical transformations.

The third project was a bit more involved than the previous two, which were required projects in a freshman fine arts course. This project took place during an intensive and extensive interim course entitled "Line." This course was suggested and initiated by our dance instructor who was joined by a visual artist and myself. Students explored the definition of line in the three areas of dance, visual arts, and music and developed a fifteen-minute, multimedia, multi-arts presentation involving the students' own work in dance, film, and music.

The students discussed "line in music," including line as melody, harmony, rhythm, timbre, texture, dynamics, and emotion. As a result of our discussions the students created their own "lines" using whatever musical resources and talents they had at their disposal. Their compositions were used as catalysts for their subsequent dances and filmmaking. Paul Klee's *The Thinking Eye*, Vasili Kandinsky's works, John Cage's *Notations*, and R. Murray Schaefer's *Creative Music Education* provided valuable ideas.

For pitch, the students drew a line indicating the shape of the pitch line in Johann Sebastian Bach's *Sonata in G-dur* for cello, the familiar prelude movement, and Edgar Varèse's *Density 21.5* for solo flute. On an 11" by 17" piece of paper with seconds marked off, they had to draw the shape of the pitch line with movement from high to low. After these two works, I played them a work of mine titled *Ruins* that used alto flute and soprano where the pitch line alternated between a single line and two contrasting lines, moving constantly back and forth from one to two lines. Finally, they looked at Bach's "Invention No. 2," in which he writes two distinct lines, one in exact canon to the other, and a movement from his *Musical Offering* where one line is free, one is the theme, and one is in strict fugal imitation.

After this discussion of pitch, they wrote a paragraph on pitch as line. One student wrote that each line of music has a distinct beginning, middle, and end. It begins on a certain point, a note, just as a line begins with a point, a dot. A note begins the piece, but it is not the whole piece. Here movement takes a part. Movement continues the piece with a succession of points or notes. Each note is its own entity, but together, these notes form a line of melody; the melody is the main part of the music. As with a drawing, music has a certain shape. The timbre, dynamics, texture, pitch, and rhythm merge with each other to give the music a soft, strong, flowing, or jagged feel. The most important factor of a piece is the melody.

After pitch, we discussed harmony as line and students listened to a twelve-bar blues, a progression of chords as vertical points on a harmonic line in which chords first move away from the tonic, creating tension, to the dominant; once the dominant is reached, movement is once again created by moving back to the tonic, or relaxed state. We looked at Bach's "Prelude in C" from *The Well-Tempered Clavier*, and we drew a line showing the harmonic line and the alteration of tension and relaxation. Finally, we looked at a brief minuet by Mozart that showed how melody and harmony combine to create a line of music. We spent less time on the other elements of music, looking at dynamics as line in Witold Lutoslawski's brief *Postlude for Orchestra*, at timbre as line in Maurice Ravel's *Bolero*, and then texture, rhythm, and emotion.

For their major project the students created a one-minute musical line concentrating on one of the elements of music, though certainly all elements would play a part. They notated their short pieces, creating a notation that would express their distinctive line. The students composed some marvelous pieces for Fisher-Price xylophone, glasses (rubbed and hit with cork mallets), Casios, classical guitar, harp, piano, and computer, and even a brief masterpiece for Hammond organ and parrot.

Finalizing the Work

We listened to all the pieces and began to "think" how we might combine these line works into an extended composition that could be danced and also provide the background for a film. We ended up expanding the classical guitar line into a three-minute piece using Orff instruments, a synthesizer, and glasses. Some line works we kept "as is," determining what sequence they would be put into the harp, computer, Hammond organ, and parrot. We mixed

some of the excerpts into a new work emphasizing the contrast of the lines, and this composite work was used as the background from the film. For the finale, we created a three-minute piece using only rhythmic lines, piling up the ostinatos into a pulsating finish.

The final fifteen-minute work was truly a multimedia and multi-arts experience (in vogue these days in light of the collaborative works of Phillip Glass and others) that combined original musical compositions with dance and film. One of the brightest and most talented students, a harp player, created two line works during the course of the four weeks. She said the course had made her "think" about composing and she really enjoyed it. She had never tried it before. On the evening of the performance, this student's parents commented that the course had gotten their daughter to compose *once again*. They explained that as a small child she had done improvising and composing and that this course had reawakened such an interest. She had been given the opportunity to explore, develop, and arouse her own attending, readiness, and desire to compose and create sound images. She didn't know that she had it in her to do so. Such an awareness and reawakening was reward enough for offering such a course.

Notes

1. Roger Sessions. *Questions About Music* (New York: W. W. Norton, 1970), 77.

2. John Cage. *Silence: Lectures and Writings* (Middletown, CT: Wesleyan University Press 1961), 191.

Alfred Balkin discusses the nine roads to discovery in this article. These nine roads are suggestions for introducing creative activities to students. Balkin also offers suggestions on obtaining student responses.

The Creative Music Classroom: Laboratory for Creativity in Life

by Alfred Balkin

• Who might have had more in common with Mozart: Stevie Wonder or Michael Jackson? Why?
• Who might have fit best into the musical life of George Washington's America: Willie Nelson, Linda Ronstadt, the Beatles, or Tina Turner? Why?
• Could Beethoven make a living in music today? How?
• What would happen to rock music if all the electricity went off?
• How could MTV be used to sell classical music?
• Imagine a conversation between Franz Schubert and Billy Joel. What would they say?

The foregoing questions are not typical of elementary music classroom instruction. Traditional American classroom pedagogy has been centered on "yessing" (giving the right answers to questions). For example, "What note is found on the first line of the treble clef staff?" E, of course, is the *only* answer. But is that learning?

In sharp contrast, creative education is built more around guessing (learning by discovery, by thought, or by intuition rather than by reflex). With this method, the teacher would say, "Here is the sound

of the note that is found on the first line of the treble clef staff. Sing what you think might be the sound of the note found on the second line, third line, space below and above the first line." This approach requires making connections, taking chances, possibly being "wrong," not being afraid to "fail," running the risk of looking or sounding foolish, seeking alternatives, making choices—discovering one's own capabilities.

This nation was conceived and realized by "guessers," those men and women who asked the "what if " questions and sought the "how to" possibilities. Yessing also had, and still has, its place, but the right answers often do not equal the most desirable learning or the most creative, effective solutions to problems. Guessers dare to be different, to be innovative, to risk. These qualities are not the exclusive domain of the world's Beethovens, da Vincis, Shakespeares, Edisons, Einsteins, and Disneys. As members of a teaching team, classroom music educators have a unique and exciting role—even an obligation—to help develop these same characteristics in children. To do this, the music teacher's technical and pedagogical skills need to be guided by some crucial philosophical principles and awarenesses about music *and* education. Consider these:

1. Music can be *the* most powerful motivating agent in a variety of learning situations.

2. It is a great responsibility to have such power, and an even greater responsibility to use it opportunely and wisely toward the all-encompassing intellectual-emotional growth of children.

Alfred Balkin is a professor of education, a composer, and the coordinator of the Integrated Creative Arts Program in the College of Education at Western Michigan University, Kalamazoo. This article originally appeared in the January 1985 Music Educators Journal.

3. Every music education experience ideally should have a dual rationale that addresses music objectives and also suggests how the attainment of those objectives might help each child deal more creatively with the world around him or her.

4. Children should be exposed to as many different kinds of music as possible. (There is an inherent lesson even in that.)

The only common criterion is that whatever music is presented be the best of its particular genre, be it classical, jazz, country, folk, or rock. There is little time or occasion for anything but the best.

All classroom experiences ideally should contribute to children's creative, cognitive, psychomotor, and affective growth. Educators generally agree that we learn most effectively through the senses, particularly in the initial stages of a learning situation. Music, because of its enjoyable, nonthreatening, equal-opportunity, emotionally satisfying nature, appeals directly to the senses. Therefore, the music classroom offers an especially healthy and amenable environment for creative development. Opportunities abound.

By design, the classroom musical experiences in this article illustrate and encourage creative characteristics and behaviors. Many music teachers already provide such experiences, but they may not perceive or present them in terms of general creative growth and contrasted to specifically musical creative growth. The connections are not automatically made by the children. The teacher's seeking and sharing those music-to-life connections is the one step beyond, perhaps the most valuable part of each music experience: the step into the Real-Life Zone. Again, it should be emphasized that some of these exercises may look familiar, but their purposes are not. It is the "how" and the "why" that make the "what" meaningful. Seeing things differently, viewing the ordinary extraordinarily, are the cornerstones of creativity. Uniqueness, though much sought after, is a bonus.

Guessing (the essence of discovery learning) has been most successful in science education. Application in music education is less frequent but equally promising. Guessing is not an end in itself, but a simple *first-stage process* to initiate creative problem solving. It is a springboard for taking chances, exercising options, and making creative choices—leading, through trial and error, to worthy, if not necessarily "correct," solutions. This musical experience uses guessing as the principal teaching technique. The second example, drawing upon the confidence gained and materials presented from the guessing experience, attempts to develop more sophisticated and creative products.

Nine Roads to Discovery

Example 1. Tell the class that you are going to create a sound using a combination of two objects that are highly visible in the room (for example, chalk and book, pencil and chalkboard, pen and desk, foot and floor, hand and chair, or finger and paper). The combinations are infinite, but can start with the obvious. Ask students to close their eyes. Ask for volunteers to imitate the sound with their voices. Tell them that their decisions should be based on thoughtful guesses. After each attempt, have the students close their eyes and repeat the original sound. Discuss the differences from one to the next in relation to the original. Ask individuals what guesses led to their sounds. Praise each response as valid, and make it clear that the "right" answer is not nearly so important here as the thoughtful guesses and many interesting new sounds that would not have been heard otherwise. If nobody duplicates the sound after a sufficient number of responses, let the class see the sound being made as well as hear it. Repeat the same experience, but this time request that each student create his or her own original sound. Emphasize possibilities in life as in music. For example, "If things don't work out the first time, try something different."

A big step in moving children toward creative enterprise is teaching them to "compose" music, and in so doing, to think like composers (who must constantly make choices, evaluate, make new choices, and—above all—work). Children need to learn that creativity is like an automobile. Inspiration may turn on the motor, like the key in the ignition, which supplies the spark; however, if there is not enough fuel in the engine to run it and get the job done, the spark is useless. Example 1 has cranked the engine. Example 2 now applies the gas pedal.

Example 2. Divide the class into groups of four. Assign each group the task of creating a thirty- to forty-five–second composition using any of the sounds from Example 1. Advise the class that new sounds may be added. Have each group arrange its sounds using principles of unity and variety to make the most interesting composition. Suggest that each group also use some changes in dynamics or tempo. Ask each group to perform its sound composition and explain how it arrived at choices. Urge the class to comment on each piece and offer suggestions for improvement. Discuss possible changes. After all the groups have evaluated the changes, ask each group to refine its composition. Make it clear that the refinement process is the *real* work of the composer and is the aspect of creativity that is the most essential and, for many, the least desirable.

Perform the revised compositions. Have the class select its favorite portions from each group composition. Using the same principles of unity and variety, restructure these various sections into one class composition lasting no more than ninety seconds. Emphasize possibilities and their relationship to the decision-making process. Draw upon Real-Life Zone connections to reinforce, stimulate, and suggest values by asking such questions as: "What if your funds were unlimited and you could buy all the stereo equipment and recordings you wanted: What items would you choose? Why? What if the situation were just the opposite and you had to save for a long time to make a purchase? What would you buy first? Why? What if you were a rock recording star—how would you keep up with your neighborhood friends?" Example 2 also involved the individual's contributing to cooperative group interaction, certainly a factor that adds a needed social dimension to a child's creative development, and one that appears in all of the remaining exercises.

Example 3. Have the class create additional compositions using strictly vocal sounds other than singing. Follow the same procedures and principles as in Example 2. Example 4 returns to thoughtful guesses of a more insightful nature than Example 1. Example 5 develops those insights through more discovery processes to create specific products.

Example 4. Ask each student to bring an empty glass or jar to class. Invite pairs of students to show their containers, and ask the class to guess which of the two, when struck, will sound higher or lower. Discuss why. After a few guesses, each of the two students will then strike their containers with a metal spoon, wooden mallet, or other beater, so that the class can hear the differences in sound. Introduce the term "pitch." After the difference in pitches has been determined, place the lower-sounding container to the left of the higher sounding one. Keep repeating this process, pair by pair, As part of the process, compare each pair to all succeeding pairs. Keep rearranging succeeding pairs. Keep rearranging the containers accordingly. Ask the class to decide which containers have the same sound. Put the extras aside after speculating as to why different-looking containers can produce the same pitch. Have students count how many *different* pitches have been discovered. (Twelve would be ideal, but is unlikely to happen on the first attempt.) Explain the chromatic scale. If those twelve sounds have not been discovered, ask students to bring another glass container different from their first. Ask *why* it should be different. Try to find the missing pitches during a follow-up lesson. Stress that trial and error is an indispensable technique in solving life's problems as well as musical problems. Ask for personal examples.

Example 5. Using the pitches of the containers in Example 4, through trial-and-error discovery, try to play a familiar song. After the class assimilates the procedure, assign small groups to discover their own familiar songs. The groups do not have to play the whole song, but only enough of it so that it is recognizable to the class.

Example 6. Tell the class that you are going to play two recordings, one of which is called "The Flight of the Bumblebee" by Nikolai Rimsky-Korsokov, and the other, *Prélude à l'après-midi d'un faune* by Claude Debussy. Let the class guess how each piece might sound in relation to tempo, rhythm, dynamics, and instrumentation. Ask what instrument they might select to play the bumblebee or the faun. Why? Discuss choices. Play the recordings and have the class comment on the differences between their guesses and the actual sounds. Present similar guessing exercises comparing and contrasting other pairs of compositions such as "Gardens in the Rain" by Debussy and "Cloudburst" from the *Grand Canyon Suite* by Ferde Grofé or "Pacific 231" by Arthur Honegger and "The Little Train of the Caipura" by Heitor Villa-Lobos. Emphasize that creative guessing is an invaluable tool in problem solving; one needn't be afraid to guess; and any good guess is a step in the right direction. Ask the class for examples of how some of their recent guesses have turned out. Discuss why they may have turned out well or badly.

Example 7. Play a short passage from a Wolfgang Amadeus Mozart symphony. Ask students in the class to guess what they might be watching on a television or movie screen as this music is playing. Ask why each student chose his or her particular scene. Repeat this exercise with recordings like these: the opening dance from Leonard Bernstein's *West Side Story*, the first movement from Ludwig van Beethoven's "Pastorale" symphony, Indian sitar music, West African vocal chants, Edgard Varèse's "Poème électronique," Modest Musorgsky's "A Night on Bald Mountain," a Gregorian chant, some Latin jazz-rock by Santana, the finale from Igor Stravinsky's "Firebird" suite, or the "Star Spangled Banner." Ask the students to recall experiences in their own lives and to decide which piece might best illustrate a particular experience. Inform them that if no music from class fits their personal television scene, they may bring some music from home that is more suitable. Approach the life experience from the opposite direction. Ask the class if any particular piece of music brought any particular personal experience to mind. If so, why? Stress the relationship of music to visual impressions, both real and imagined. Discuss how music can bring past events and feelings to mind.

Example 8. This experience involves the class composing a song. Though the class will select its own subject for this exercise, let's assume they have chosen spring. once again, this experience also emphasizes possibilities, alternatives, and decision making; but it basically revolves around *making connections*.

Ask the class to think about events, sounds, sights, pleasures, sports, and other concepts dealing with spring. Write all the responses on the chalkboard or overhead projector transparency. Let the class decide which ideas it wants to pursue. Ask for phrases to describe the ideas. Put them into some coherent order that is agreeable to the class. Decide upon a rhyme scheme if the class chooses to compose a rhyming song. (Songs that rhyme tend to have more immediate appeal and memorability than those that do not. Children love rhymes, even complex ones.) Introduce the class to the rhyming dictionary as a tool (like a thesaurus) that not only provides many more rhymes than we would think of, but more importantly, triggers new ideas and new connections and even helps professional composers to create more interesting songs.

Guide the class to refine each line to its satisfaction. After the song poem has been accepted by the class, encourage the students to sing musical phrases to accompany the words of each line. Tape-record each student's contribution, and ask the class to decide which musical phrases best suit each line of the song's lyrics. Put the entire song on the board or an overhead projector. Record the class singing the entire song. Devise an attractive piano, guitar, or classroom instrument accompaniment. Review and refine. Stress the "re" factor: refine, review, redo, revise, rearrange, repair, rethink, restructure, reorder, replay, repeat, redefine, and so on. Make it clear that creative products may start with divine inspiration, but only dedication and hard work can bring an inspiration to fruition. Reinforcement of this concept in an educational setting may have a major impact on the child's life.

Example 9. Ask students to recall experiences in which they were afraid to look foolish, act differently, or take a chance. Discuss these experiences and accompanying feelings. Share some of your own. Play a recording with a strong, steady beat. Ask the class to move as a group according to those body movements specified by the teacher. Now ask for volunteers to keep the beat using their own special movements. Do some yourself as examples. Emphasize that so long as students keep the beat, all responses are welcomed. Have students strive to make their movements different from one another's. Emphasize that this is a worthwhile, creative, and pleasurable experience in which sharing, taking chances, not being afraid to look foolish, and being one's self are what the lesson is all about. After the successful completion of this exercise, ask students to recall other situations in which they did take chances. Again share some of your own.

How the teacher makes the *life* connections within the context of the music lesson, by seizing the teachable moment, is personal and a manifestation of the teacher's own creativity and style. It should always be borne in mind that music is just *one* medium that makes a contribution to the education of the whole child. Once the music teacher begins thinking primarily in terms of how music can promote creative growth in life, the teacher's own creativity will bloom and lead to new learning experiences that will actively foment children's taking chances, exploring possibilities, making choices, seeing things differently, not being afraid to be "wrong," exercising options, finding connections, making thoughtful decisions, realizing the value of trial-and-error learning, guessing—not simply yessing. The teacher will constantly be mindful of music learning's relationship to life, and make those concrete connections to life in a positive, enthusiastic, resourceful, and creative manner. The complex problems we now face will only be solved by enlightened creative thinking.

The movers of tomorrow are the guessers in our classrooms today. We must recognize them, uncover more, and give them every opportunity to flourish, for the sake of us all.

In this article, Saul Feinberg offers practical suggestions on helping students develop creative abilities through listening experience. The step-by-step process is clearly defined and presented and should be of use to all readers.

Creative Problem-Solving and the Music Listening Experience

by Saul Feinberg

The one learning experience that best reflects the significant changes that have occurred in music education over the past decade is listening. Taken out of the passive, rather perfunctory role it played in former days, listening has been elevated to a position where its true function in music and general education can at last be realized. This function, essentially, is to serve as a means by which all individuals can respond aesthetically to what is expressive in music.

Such conferences as the Yale Seminar in Music Education, the Tanglewood Symposium, the institutes for the Contemporary Music Project, and more recently, the Conference for Advanced Placement in Music have consistently emphasized the importance of listening courses in helping both the performer and the nonperformer deal more perceptively and affectively with music. They have also called for approaches that can make these learning experiences more dynamic and more creative. Paradoxically, however, while the purposes and values of aesthetically oriented courses in music have been dealt with in deep and penetrating ways, the means by which these goals can actually be realized in the classroom have been given only minimal attention by the profession.

The reasons for this gap between the philosophy and the practices of aesthetic education become clear

Saul Feinberg teaches music at Lincoln High School, Philadelphia, Pennsylvania. This article originally appeared in the September 1974 Music Educators Journal.

when we realize that many music educators are still using rather limited strategies and activities to deal with one of humanity's most complex and revealing phenomena—the aesthetic experience. These approaches include those that emphasize the programmatic, nonmusical aspects of music and those that concentrate too much on the factual content of music. What is needed is an approach to aesthetic listening that not only enables students to learn *about* music but also encourages them to respond intellectually and affectively to the creative process that produced it. Such a multifaceted approach—an approach that is close to both the creative process and the *created* product (the music)—can be properly called a "creative problem-solving approach."

Essentially, a creative approach to perceptive listening involves the setting up of problem-solving situations in which the listener can function as both a *thinker* (a problem-solver) and a *learner* (a gainer of knowledge). In such a setting, students are not told what is significant in a piece of music, nor are they informed as to what is happening in the work. Rather, they are given opportunities to explore these possibilities for themselves through the working out of various problems and hypotheses. Such an analytical approach enables students to think in the manner of a composer as well as that of a listener. In such roles, they are able to share some of the problems faced by the composer and to respond to the work's aesthetic qualities in a deep and penetrating way. A creative problem-solving approach can do more than merely teach "content." While students are learning fundamental ideas about music, they can also cultivate those behaviors of thinking and listening that will promote a pattern of continuous aesthetic and creative growth. Certainly, such a "product" as this represents the ultimate goal of all aesthetic music education programs.

If this creative approach is based on the belief that students can develop intellectual abilities at the same time they are acquiring knowledge, the question can be asked "What abilities?" Fortunately, answers to this question have come out of the extensive research that has taken place over the past two decades in the area of creative behavior. So revealing have the results of this research been that they have implications not only for disciplines naturally linked with the creative process—such as those in art education—but for all the subject areas in general education.

Of central importance have been the changing beliefs about the nature and nurturing of creative potential. In sharp contrast to the earlier viewpoint that creativeness is a quality reserved only for the gifted few, today it is seen as a quality that all individuals possess in some degree—a quality that each person has the democratic *right* and the psychological *need* to develop. Through the pioneering efforts of such creative psychologists as J. P. Guilford, P. R. Merrifield, and E. Paul Torrance, specific behaviors of problem solving and creative thinking have been delineated that can be significantly improved when appropriate conditions for their development are made available. Most of these creative-thinking abilities have been identified from the extensive studies with Guilford's extraordinary model of human intelligence—the structure-of-intellect model. In this model, Guilford and his associates have been able to hypothesize 120 intellectual abilities, each of which has its own distinctive quality. Ninety-eight of these abilities have already been demonstrated through a complex system of factor analysis.[1]

Although it is conceivable that all of the intellectual abilities theorized in the structure-of-intellect model could be dealt with in some way in a creative listening approach, the abilities most compatible with such an approach are those classified under the operation labeled "divergent production." In contrast to the other "thinking" processes in the model, this operation is concerned with generating solutions to a problem that are both useful and innovative. Since divergent production involves the bringing together of previously unrelated ideas to arrive at a solution, it is the cognitive process most identified with creative thinking. The "divergent thinking" abilities most important for a creative approach to perceptive music listening are fluency, flexibility, and elaboration.

In terms of general intellectual functioning, *fluency* is concerned with the ability to generate a quantity of adaptable (but not necessarily original) solutions to a problem within a certain amount of time. In many tests for fluent thinking, the individual is asked to describe as many uses as possible for a particular object—for example, a hammer. The more solutions the individual is able to produce, the higher the fluency score would be. This ability can be related to perceptive music listening by asking the listener to tell how many different ways a particular music idea is used in a piece of music. The more "uses" perceived, the more fluent is the listening. Here are several examples of listening tasks that require fluent thinking abilities (suggestions for specific compositions or ideas that can be used are enclosed in parentheses):

1. Before listening to the following music example (the opening section from Schubert's *Symphony No. 5* in B-flat), describe the different ways you think the main motif could be used in the music.

2. Three different themes will be played for you. After listening to them, pick out two that you think were written by the same composer and explain how they are related.

3. I will play two themes for you. If you were asked to compose a bridge connecting these two themes, how would you organize such a passage?

Flexibility, as a divergent thinking behavior, is concerned with generating many different kinds of logical solutions to a problem. Although this behavior is closely linked with fluency, it is involved more with how many changes or alternative means were used to solve the problem than with the quantity of responses. Flexibility implies openness and originality. In terms of perceptive music listening, flexibility involves tasks that ask the listener to indicate the different ways in which music ideas are changed and combined in a piece of music. The more "fixated" the listener is on any one element in the music, such as rhythm, the less he is able to respond as a flexible listener. Here are three examples of listening tasks that call for flexible thinking:

certo for Orchestra), describe what you think the second conductor did that was different from what the first conductor did. Which version did you find more satisfying? Why?

Elaboration is the creative thinking behavior concerned with generating step-by-step procedures to solve a particular problem. Again, the more useful and original the solution, the more creative is the thinking expressed. Relating elaborative thinking to perceptive music listening involves tasks in which the listener indicates procedures needed to carry out various ideas through music. Here are two examples:

1. Listen to the music up to...(the gong at the end of Tchaikovsky's *Symphony No. 2* in C minor (["Little Russian"]). Keeping in mind what you have

1. After listening to the following composition ("Chester" from Schuman's *New England Triptych*), make up a series of questions that you think relate to what you heard. Remember, the more areas you touch on in your questions, the more flexible you are thinking.

2. While listening to the following work (the second movement of Hindemith's *Symphonic Metamorphosis of Themes by Weber)*, place a check after any of the music qualities listed on your "Aural Flexibility List" (see figure 1) whenever they reappear in the music. Each section will be indicated to you. Don't get "stuck" on any one quality.

3. After listening to two different recordings of the same composition (the finale from Bartók's Con-

Music Qualities	Sections in the Music									
	1	2	3	4	5	6	7	8	9	10
a change in tempo										
a melody in low register										
melody against melody										
thick, dissonant chords										
a crescendo										
a sudden change in volume										
a solo wind instrument										
a percussion instrument										
pizzicato										
a new theme										
a return to the "A" theme										
a question-answer effect										
number of qualities heard										

Total

Figure 1. Aural Flexibility List

heard, describe how you would bring this work to an end.

2. Refer to your "Music Qualities List" (see figure 2) and write down the number of those qualities you think could be used to depict each of the following scenes (an approaching storm, the storm itself, the end of the storm). While listening to this selection (the fourth movement from Beethoven's *Symphony No. 6* in F major), circle the numbers of those qualities that were used by the composer to give an impression in music of these scenes. (This type of musical "Bingo" activity could be adapted to numerous other elaborative listening tasks concerned with describing various music forms and contemporary styles.)

RHYTHM	1.	Steady pulse	**DYNAMICS**	23.	Gradually louder
	2.	Irregular pulse		24.	Gradually softer
	3.	No pulse		25.	Suddenly loud
	4.	Generally slow tempo		26.	Suddenly soft
	5.	Generally fast tempo		27.	Many dynamic changes
	6.	Gradually slower		28.	Few dynamic changes—generally soft
	7.	Gradually faster		29.	Few dynamic changes—generally loud
	8.	A sudden change in tempo	**TONE COLOR**	30.	Solo tone colors
MELODY	9.	Generally a stepwise melody		31.	Small performance group (fewer than fifteen)
	10.	A very jumpy melody		32.	Large performance group (more than fifteen)
	11.	A simple, songlike melody		33.	Electronic sounds
	12.	A very elaborate melody		34.	Pizzicato effects
	13.	Melodic ornaments (trills, mordents)		35.	Cymbal crash
HARMONY	14.	Generally traditional harmonies		36.	Drum rolls
	15.	Many dissonant harmonies		37.	Traditional tone colors
	16.	A "key" feeling (tonal)		38.	Unusual tone colors
	17.	No feeling of "key" (atonal)		39.	Very high or low registers
	18.	Shifting "key" feeling (modulation)	**FORM**	40.	Balanced ideas
	19.	Same texture throughout—generally thin		41.	Many repeated ideas
	20.	Same texture throughout—generally thick		42.	Question-answer effect
	21.	Homophonic texture (melody against chords)		43.	Only one section
	22.	Polyphonic texture (melody against melody)		44.	Two or more sections (or themes)
				45.	"Freely" organized

Figure 2. Music Qualities List

A Preparational Listening Lesson

Problem: To have the students realize the importance of being open and flexible when listening to music.

Preparational activities:
Familiarize the class with the following motif (from the third movement of Bartók's *Music for Strings, Percussion, and Celesta*):

Play a recording of the music and ask the class to listen for the motif.

Have the individual students describe what they heard. Make note of some of the ideas they may have missed, such as the motif being repeated more than ten times; the motif being played backwards (retrograde); the motif being repeated twice as fast and twice as slow (diminution and augmentation); and the motif being played as a question-answer effect.

Ask the class why they did not detect all of these ideas. Lead to the realization that most of the students were unable to recognize these things (and others) in the music because they were limiting their *listening* to only the general sounds of the orchestra.

Exploratory-transformative activities:
Emphasize the necessity of going beyond what is obvious or familiar by giving the students a divergent-thinking problem to solve, such as the following:

How many squares do you see? (By shifting one's perceptions, it is possible to count thirty squares of varying sizes.)

Replay the Bartók example to give students an opportunity to listen more divergently this time. Ask the class to indicate other qualities they were able to perceive in the music. Replay the example to amplify the responses.

Synthetic activities:
Apply the realizations about "divergent listening" by having the class describe what they hear in another work (the third movement from Brahms' *Symphony No. 4* in E minor, Op. 98).

Pose such "test" questions as these: Who can clap the rhythm of the main motif? Who can hum it? Who can play it on the piano? How many times was it repeated? How was it changed (inverted, played in a low register, played pizzicato, played in minor, and so on)?

Re-emphasize the idea that the perceptive music listener is one who is open and flexible in his or her listening.

Figure 3.

Considering the complexity of creative thinking and the multiplicity of ways to approach creative teaching, you could easily wonder how it is possible to translate all these factors into a problem of meaningful teaching-learning experiences. Once again, however, a solution to the problem can be found in the results of research into creative behavior. A model for structuring a creative problem-solving approach can be identified in the very process of creative thinking itself. This process has been described in many different ways by many different scholars. All of these diversified descriptions, however, tend to hypothesize the creative-thinking process as consisting of three interrelated stages—a *preparational stage* in which a problem is perceived, identified, and prepared for some kind of solution (problem-solving activity cannot occur until a gap in information is sensed by the individual); an *exploratory-transformative stage* in which possible answers to the problem are explored and gradually transformed into some kind of solution (the longer the search is sustained, the richer and more creative the solution is likely to be); and a *synthetic stage* in which the solution is evaluated and internalized for future learning tasks (the ultimate result being further learning and growth for the individual).

This preparation-exploratory-transformative-synthetic sequence of problem-solving can serve as a model for many different experiences in a music listening course. It can be used to structure individual lessons, to unify several different lessons, or to organize a series of interrelated lessons made up of "listening episodes." What is basically involved in all of these structures is a series of preparational activities in which specific problems relating to a music idea or a specific work of music can be identified, a series of exploratory-transformative activities in which many different kinds of solutions can be generated through creative problem-solving experiences with the elements and the processes of the music being explored (it is in this stage that all of the divergent thinking abilities described earlier could be utilized), and a series of synthetic activities in which understandings and skills learned from the problem-solving experience can become internalized and applied to new listening tasks.

It is interesting to realize not only that the tripartite design of creative thinking is an appropriate model for organizing the lessons of a listening episode but also that it can serve as a means by which the entire listening course can be structured. Such a plan would consist of three developmental phases—a preparational phase, an exploratory-transformative phase, and a synthetic phase.

In the *preparational phase* of the course, the prime objective is to establish a level of openness and flexibility on the part of students that will enable them to cope with increasingly more complex and sophisticated kinds of listening tasks. This phase of the course is particularly important because its purpose is to formulate an attitudinal frame of reference that is sufficiently divergent to sustain a pattern of continuous learning throughout the course (and perhaps, beyond). From the various lessons in the preparational phase, it is hoped that the students will come to realize and accept the following basic guidelines for becoming a more perceptive music listener:

- Try to give your full attention to the music being heard.
- Focus on the various elements that make up the music.
- Be open to new listening experiences, not "blinded" by past habits.
- Postpone your judgment of the music until it has been fully experienced.
- Listen to the music many times.

An example of a preparational listening lesson structured along the lines of the creative-thinking model is described in figure 3.

In the *exploratory-transformative phase* of the course, the behaviors of perceptive music listening and creative problem-solving gradually merge into a totally integrated process. The primary objective of the listening episodes in this phase is to provide opportunities for students to develop their listening abilities and understandings through direct and prolonged encounters with complete works of music. Although survey lessons can be used to develop various music concepts and skills, the approach most compatible with the highly integrated nature of creative thinking is one that encourages the listener to become involved with the music elements and processes of *complete* pieces of music. When such an approach is taken, it is possible for the listener not only to share some of the creative problems that the composer faced when writing the work but also to experience the work as a complete, integrated whole. It is through this bringing together of the various parts previously explored that a type of musical gestalt can occur, and a more revealing aesthetic experience can take place. The dynamics of such an "aesthetic-whole" approach has been described eloquently by Edmund Feldman: *The final meaning and the entire funding of meaning does not take place until the work of art has been experienced in its fullness and entirety.* Until then, the perceptions are separate and the meanings provisional. Not until the whole work is experienced can the interactions among the parts take place, the sense of wholeness be achieved, and the heightening and intensification of perception be felt.[2]

Although there is a definite need for more listening materials that can help students interact more perceptively and creatively with complete works of music, several student-oriented materials have been developed. These include those by Bennett Reimer,[3] by the Yale Music Curriculum Project,[4] and by me.[5]

In the culminating phase of the course, the *synthetic phase*, students are given opportunities to integrate their listening behaviors and understandings by applying them to tasks that call for responses that involve synthesizing. In this stage of perceptive music listening development, students are encouraged to make aesthetic judgments when verbalizing about creative processes in music, when offering criticisms about specific works and performance interpretations, when distinguishing works that are banal from those that demonstrate creativity, and when formulating original listening guides and analyses of works of music. From these final, evaluative experiences, students should come to realize that the listening experience symbolizes a unique encounter with the human condition, an experience that grows and deepens as individuals themselves also grow and deepen.

Although the main objective of this article has been to describe an approach to music listening that can bring a greater compatibility between the goals and practices of aesthetic education, there has been a larger intent as well. This is to emphasize once again that music is not just an entertaining "thing" to have around when "important" things are finished. It can also make a unique and significant contribution to one of general education's most valued goals—helping each person become all that he or she can be, a fully thinking, knowing, and feeling individual.

Notes

1. A comprehensive discussion of this model and its three-dimensional design can be found in J. P. Guilford's *The Nature of Human Intelligence* (New York: McGraw-Hill Book Company, 1967) and in Guilford and Ralph Hoepfner's *The Analysis of Intelligence* (New York: McGraw-Hill Book Company, 1971).

2. Edmund B. Feldman, "The Nature of the Aesthetic Experience," in *Report of the Commission on Art Education* edited by Jerome J. Hausman (Washington, DC: National Art Education Association, 1965), p. 36.

3. Bennett Reimer, *Development and Trial in a Junior and Senior High School of a Two-Year Curriculum in General Music*, Project No. H-116 (Washington, DC: U.S. Office of Education, 1967).

4. Kenneth A. Wendrick and Claude V. Palisca, *An Approach to Musical Understanding for Secondary School Students, Report of the Yale Music Curriculum Project*, Project No. 221, U.S. Office of Education (New Haven, CT: Yale University, 1970).

5. Saul Feinberg, *Blueprints for Musical Understanding*, Four Series (New York: Warner Bros. Publications, Inc., 1964, 1971).

In this article, Thomas A. Regelski discusses the use of sound compositions in the enhancement of individual creativity. He states that sound compositions involve composing, performing, and listening—three important activities that should be included in curricular offerings.

A Sound Approach to Sound Composition

by Thomas A. Regelski

The sound composition, or soundscape, has proven a valid educational technique in a number of countries.[1] This type of composition consists of sounds not usually associated with music, and often generated by nontraditional instruments and sound sources, but organized and arranged according to formal and expressive ends and purposes that *are* associated with music. Although some characterize soundscapes as programmatic in inspiration, if not necessarily so in effect, sound composition involves all the processes associated with traditional conceptions of vocal and instrumental music. However, avant-garde and nontraditional approaches to music can also be addressed through this teaching medium, which makes it an ideal vehicle to prepare composers, performers, and listeners for the ever-evolving music of the future.

Because sound compositions require no prior mastery of any particular sound medium or notational system, and because they draw the attention of students to the expressiveness of all sonorous possibilities, they allow students almost immediate access to the compositional dimension of musical experience. Insights gained as to what compositional activity involves and makes available thus complement experiences unique to listening and performing—the other two prime forms of musical functioning. Having gained impetus through the efforts of R. Murray Schafer, John and Elizabeth Paynter, Peter Aston, George Self, and the Manhattanville Music Curriculum Project, the sound composition technique still needs some clarification in ordinary classrooms with ordinary schoolchildren.

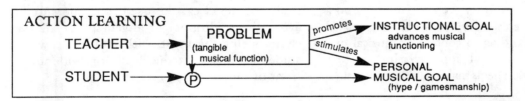

Figure 1. With action learning, the tangible musical function brought into focus in the compositional problem *(P)* devised by the teacher becomes the student's conscious musical goal. The hype or gamesmanship may initially capture students' imaginations, but done properly, this eliciting of interest is intrinsic or contributes to intrinsically musical ends. The sense of relevance contributed when students are allowed choices concerning certain limitations also stimulates acceptance of the teacher-set problem as their own personal goal for the moment, while the musical challenges of the specified limitations directly promote the teacher's instructional goals for advancing one or more musical functions. These limitations thus provide the teacher with specific control over the direction and nature of the skills, understandings, and attitudes elicited and improved.

Thomas A. Regelski is chairman of the music education division of the School of Music, State University College, Fredonia, New York. This article originally appeared in the May 1986 Music Educators Journal.

The General Approach

Some teachers use sound composition merely as an activity; in such cases, the process of composition may be modeled to some degree and students actively entertained musically, but little tangible or long-lasting learning results. Other teachers treat sound composition as a "unit," studied for a limited time but not integrated with other listening, performing, and compositional experiences. Such a lockstep approach seldom benefits any type of musical instruction, and it is no more effective with sound compositions. While sound composition can also be used to "teach creativity," this end is best approached as a natural by-product of composition rather than the focus of such instruction, if only because no one has much of an idea what creativity is. At best, starting out to teach an unknown leads to all kinds of hit-or-miss results; at worst, it makes a mockery of the craft of composition.

Because sound compositions involve composing, performing, *and* listening, they are among the most efficient and effective of all instructional tools. The ability to synthesize all phases of musical involvement makes sound compositions versatile as introductions or follow-ups to other significant musical involvements, as well as worthy emphases in their own right. Rather than being treated as self-sufficient ends—the "activities" approach—or being confined to only a small portion of a course of study—the "unit" approach—they are best employed on a regular basis, intermixed with other kinds of related experiences, according to content or musical process—the so-called spiral approach. In this way, sound composition helps make natural and continu-ing connections with other types of learning experiences.

An "action learning" approach takes the "spiral" process one step further, using sound compositions as instructional tools for content tangibly related to students' potential musical involvement outside of school or after graduation.[2] Action learning also strives to derive much of what will be expressed musically through sound-composing activities from students' present lives and experiences. Not until students have had significant experience attempting to render personal ideas, experiences, and feelings in terms of organized sound structures can a teacher expect them to respect the process of composition and the role of a composer. And without this basis, listening and performing experiences become abstract, irrelevant, and boring!

Arranging the Classroom

Like most student-focused activities, sound compositions are best mounted in a classroom with the chairs arranged in an open circle, horseshoe, V, or any other such shape that creates an open space that functions somewhat like a stage. In such an arrangement, students can see and hear each other in discussion, and the teacher's importance as a focal point is diminished, in favor of the students' own interactions with the teacher's guidance. If the class is large, a double row of chairs or desks can be used, but one should avoid the traditional arrangement of all the chairs facing the front, with multiple rows of students looking at the heads of students in front of them.

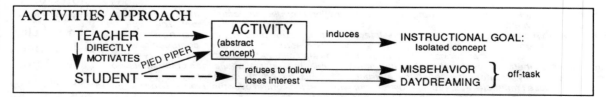

Figure 2. Here, the teacher's short-term instructional goal is to teach an abstract concept. But because a lifeless abstraction cannot intrinsically promote or stimulate acceptance by students as their own personal musical goal, the teacher must directly motivate the class; the students more or less willingly, but blindly, follow the lead of the teacher as their main conscious goal of the moment. Hence their willingness to participate depends largely on the immediate entertainment value of the activity and its implementation by a personable teacher (the "Pied Piper"). At best, what is learned is a verbal abstraction (discursive understanding) or some incremental or short-term gain in an atomistic skill. However, often students may refuse to pursue the enticements of the teacher or may lose interest quickly, resulting in off-task daydreaming or misbehavior.

To reduce confusion at the start of the class, arrange the chairs or desks into small groups, as widely separated as space allows, before class begins. This avoids interactions and interferences between groups. As students enter the room, they should immediately go to their assigned group. However, during performance of student works, the open "stage" arrangement is preferred. Also, avoid having all the instruments or other sound sources gathered in one small corner or closet. This prevents "traffic jams" when students go to choose instruments. It is best if the sound sources are on open shelving where students can see them and can plan many of their sounds without first having to experiment actively with each instrument.

Problem Solving

The key to organizing lesson content—what is to be learned—lies in the stating of a *problem* for composition. Such a learning problem presents a goal to be reached (the composition) according to a variety of requirements and restrictions (the *limitations* that make it a problem). From the point of view of action learning, it is helpful if the teacher organizes a problem either modeled on some real-life experience or in some other way related to the students' lives. An example of the former would be a sound composition in AB form, with one section based on a trip to the dentist's office and the other on the feelings experienced at a party; an example of the latter would be a similar composition based on emotions with which students can identify. This is not to say that sound compositions should always be "program" music, but it helps if the assigned problem finds its inspiration for musical expression in a connection to real life. In fact, one thing learned very quickly is how poorly music provides literal descriptions of the intended points of departure.

The *limitations* accompanying the problem function somewhat for the teacher as do the variables of a science experiment for a scientist. In fact, it is useful to think of these musical problems as experiments that test the student's hypotheses—in this case, their compositions—by producing observable results. The kind of limitations the teacher sets is what makes creativity and learning possible. Without limits, the student has too many places to begin, too many directions in which to go, but teacher-imposed limitations focus attention on relevant musical variables. Thus, sound compositions do not teach *concepts*, because concepts are ongoing processes, not finished products. Instead, sound composition evokes *conception* in those functional areas of musical learning the teacher wishes to advance.

A problem, then, is stated entirely in terms of limitations. A sample problem might be

> An ABA composition
> Approximately 10 seconds per section
> Showing the students' musical interpretation of two contrasting feelings, such as happy-sad or tense-relaxed
> Using only metallic, glass, and ceramic sounds

With such limitations, students focus on expressive contrasts and musical variables other than timbre, such as pitch, duration, and intensity. If an assignment allowed the use of any sound source but limited students only to a mezzo piano or mezzo forte dynamic range, a somewhat different set of variables and, therefore, different learning would be involved.

It generally helps if students are allowed a significant degree of free choice in key dimensions or parameters within the limitations. In the earlier example, for instance, they can freely choose the pair of contrasting feelings that serves as the expressive basis for their composition. Such a choice provides a self-imposed focus and becomes a personally relevant goal. Being *their* goal, it is thus more motivating. (See figures 1 and 2.) In any event, such a self-set goal or limitation becomes a major criterion by which the teacher, the audience of classmates, and the composers evaluate the composition and performance. Any key choices students can be allowed to make will contribute greatly to the purposefulness with which they ultimately complete the project.

One major aspect of content not present in the earlier example, but one that must be specified as a limitation, is whether or not to notate. A soundscape can be fully notated, fully improvised, or a "planned improvisation." Fully notated compositions are the strongest, because all of their dimensions and details can be controlled by standard or invented graphic notation. However, they take much longer to complete and consume large amounts of classroom time. Fully improvised compositions, on the other hand, are the most efficient in use of class time but the least beneficial in terms of ultimate compositional control. However, they do put a premium on the need for performers to listen to one another in bringing about the desired results. "Planned improvisations" represent a compromise: Some standard or original graphic notation controls the location, nature, and degree of improvisation. With a planned improvisation, results are more predictable and may even be repeatable or—the real challenge—performable by musicians other than the composers. This type of composition makes the best use of time and focus; perhaps 50 percent of all sound compositions should be planned improvisations.

Playful Planning

"Hyping" the problem presents it in a way that stimulates the students' imaginations, especially those of preadolescents and early adolescents. The hype should not be an out-and-out lie; a good hype is believable enough to elicit students' cooperation. For example, the teacher might play a cassette tape of the teacher's own absolutely terrible, awful, stupid sound composition—made especially for the hype—and say, "I was going to send my tape to (name of a record company), but I thought this class should hear it first. Now that you say you think it stinks, I'll give you the chance to prove you can do better. Maybe I'll send a tape of your compositions instead!"

The use of "gamesmanship" is also recommended, especially if no hype is involved. Gamesmanship implies a gamelike outcome. Two things make games interesting: *fixed rules* and *indeterminate outcomes*. In the example given earlier, gamesmanship might be added at the point when the composing group tells the teacher which set of contrasting feelings has served as the basis for their composition. The teacher then writes this pair and two other pairs of contrasting feelings on the chalkboard, and the audience is asked to determine from the composition which pair of feelings, in which order, was actually used.

This type of challenge brings about several positive effects. First, each composing group will try its best to do a good job. Second, it keeps students quieter within groups during composing because they will not wish to "give away" the answer. Third, it occupies and focuses the audience's listening and attention. And, last, it serves as a basis for discussion after each piece. Unlike a real game, however, gamesmanship should not lead to winners and losers, so competition must not be emphasized; both gamesmanship and hype should be treated playfully.

Problem Solving in Stages

The phase of *planning* I call staging—not to be confused with the *physical* staging of the ultimate performance of a composition—is the most important. No matter how well planned everything else may be, if a lesson is not well-staged it will not be a success—not as concerns learning and, especially, not as concerns student behavior.

Staging takes its name from a problem-solving approach that contends that most problems can be seen as a composite of two or more smaller problems. (See figure 3.) In arriving at the overall solution, each of these smaller problems must be tackled and solved one stage at a time. In the earlier example, the teacher might present the problem to the class as comprising the following stages:

1. First, decide which pair of feelings you will use.
2. Next, plan the kinds of sounds to use for the feeling that serves as your first section.
3. Experiment with those sounds and organize your first section.
4. Plan the kinds of sounds to use for your next section; make sure you have enough contrast!
5. Explore those sounds and organize that section.
6. Decide how you are going to handle your last section. Will it be an exact

repetition of the first, or will it be recognizably similar but different in some way?

7. Organize that section.

8. Now, rehearse the whole thing. Remember, a composition has no existence apart from performance, so only a good performance represents your musical ideas well.

This is not the only way of staging the activity; it could even be broken down into smaller stages. For example, students could rehearse sections A and B together after B is completed in order to review A in memory and to insure that they can get from A to B smoothly, or to do the same for section B and the second section A.

It is always better to have too many stages than too few; the teacher can always leave some out if things are going smoothly. Also, each stage must be strictly limited as to the time available for completion. This, along with the staging of problems, could be displayed on the chalkboard or on a sheet of directions given to each group. But the teacher also should announce at the beginning of each stage, "You have three minutes to plan this section"—or whatever. When periods longer than five minutes are given, it is wise to announce periodically, "you have X minutes remaining." Without these limitations and reminders students will waste time; limiting the time focuses and increases their effort.

While students are engaged in each stage, the teacher should visit each group, informally checking student progress, monitoring behavior, and otherwise assisting if need be with small confusions and making other suggestions as may be useful. If extensive help is needed by groups, the problem is too difficult or confusing; backtrack and review as soon as possible. The teacher must also have in mind ideas for keeping faster groups productive when they finish in advance of slower groups.

It is important always to audiotape each and every sound composition. Among other things, it makes the performers more serious about their performances (for instance, not giggling extraneously) and keeps the audience quieter and more respectful. The tapes can also be played—as a motivator or part of gamesmanship—on other occasions or with other classes.

Scheduling

The timing of the soundscape process is crucial. Most sound composition projects cannot be completed, from presentation of the problem through performance of all groups, in a single class period. The teacher, then, must decide whether to begin a class period with the project and spend the entire period on the compositions or to begin class with other preliminaries—perhaps a listening lesson related to the sound composition to follow. Also, where to break the staging into two or three self-contained segments must be determined. Each of these segments must begin with adequate time to review and rehearse what was accomplished the previous time. And, of course, no portion of a sound composition project should consume more time overall than students' interest and attention spans allow.

Since teachers are likely not to be very efficient in staging their first few sound compositions—it takes practice—they should plan them to be short; then the realities of the classroom will not extend them to boring lengths. As the teacher gains expertise with staging, the scope and length of sound composition projects can be extended—at least to the judged limits of the ability of a class for extended, semi-independent effort.

Follow-up

The performance of every composing group should be discussed in terms of the musical variables the teacher focused upon in the limitations. One purpose of discussion is to bring various ideas and observations to the attention of students that will form their choices and decisions for subsequent sound compositions. It is important, thus, to elicit as wide a discussion as possible. Responses also provide tangible evidence for the teacher of the nature, level, and adequacy of students' conceptual understanding and perceptual acuity.

Discussion time should be accounted for in planning the activity. The teacher must also decide whether to discuss each composition immediately after its performance, to wait until two or three groups have performed their compositions before discussing each, or to discuss all compositions, one

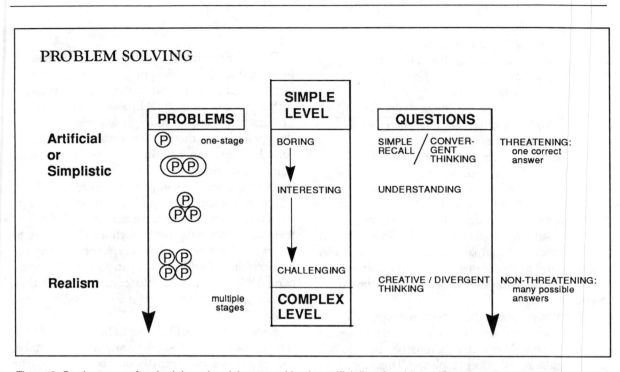

Figure 3. Students are often both bored and threatened by the artificiality of problems (P) or questions that are so simple in focus as to involve only simple recall of information or convergent thinking in pursuit of "the" correct answer. The kinds of problems that will be faced outside of and after graduation from school are seen by students as more realistic. Such problems are naturally more complex and involve multiple stages or steps to solve. Such realistic problems—and questions that foster imaginative, divergent thinking—are also less threatening and may be more interesting or challenging. But they must be within the present abilities of students and need to be accepted by students as leading to an increased ability to understand or deal with life-like musical applications about which they presently care.

at a time, after they have all been heard. Each approach has advantages and disadvantages: the first is the most effective in terms of learning but is the least time-efficient; the last uses the least time but relies too much on memory—but this is where tapes can be helpful. The middle approach is often a good compromise of effectiveness and efficiency.

The transition to the next activity should also be taken into consideration, as should the relation of the present sound composition activity to what has preceded. While each lesson or activity need not lead directly to the next, there always should be some orderly overall structure and connection between activities—in the mind of the teacher, and, if instruction is successful, in the minds of the students. It is often advisable to precede or follow a sound composition activity with a related listening lesson focusing on

the same musical problem or handling of musical variables as the sound composition.

Well Worth the Effort

Finally, the teacher is forewarned that, as with any other phase of teaching, it takes considerable practice before the teacher can effectively use this teaching tool. But because sound compositions involve composing, performing, and listening, all in one package, they are the most unified and efficient of teaching approaches, and thus they are worth the time and effort to practice until they can be mounted effectively.

Notes

1. For more information on sound composition, see Thomas A. Regelski, *Teaching General Music: Action Learning for Middle and Secondary Schools* (New York:

Schirmer, 1981) and R. Murray Schaefer, *Creative Music Education* (New York: Schirmer, 1976) and *The New Soundscape: A Handbook for the Modern Music Teacher* (Ontario, Canada: Don Mills, 1969).

2. See Regelski, *Teaching General Music;* "Action Learning," Music Educators Journal 69, no. 6 (February 1983), 46; and "Action Learning versus the Pied Piper Approach," *Music Educators Journal* 69, no. 8 (April 1983), 55.

Arthur Welwood addresses the topic of improvisation with what are sometimes called "found sounds." Although all the articles in this book are valuable in helping individuals develop creative and improvisational skills, Welwood's discussion captures the essence of improvisation in music.

Improvisation with Found Sounds

by Arthur Welwood

Making a work of music is not difficult, and composition is one area of the arts in which students often seem to be vitally interested. Composing and improvising music should be as routine as writing an English composition, giving an extemporaneous talk, or learning one's multiplication tables. The goal should not be to create masterpieces but to become involved in the creative selection and arrangement of music materials and to develop skills in self-evaluation and constructive self-criticism.

Found Instruments

An effective approach to teaching composition is through improvisation with "found" instruments. A found instrument is any ready-made object that is capable of producing a sound and that has been discovered (or found) to be musically valuable. Such methods of playing as striking, blowing, rubbing, scratching, shaking, plucking, or dropping serve to classify found instruments into aerophones (wind types), chordophones (stringed types), membranophones (drum-head types), and idiophones (types that are shaken, rubbed, or struck). A found instrument differs from a conventional one in that it is usually simpler in construction and its ready-made form is not usually associated with the music of a particular culture.

Arthur Welwood formerly was associate professor of music at Central Connecticut State College in New Britain. The article orginally appreared in the January 1980 Music Educators Journal.

In working with heterogeneous classes of students at the beginning stages of composition and improvisation, it is preferable to use primitive and seemingly unsophisticated ready-made objects. Because they are not normally used in music-making, their sound possibilities are, to some extent, unknown, and students can search out their musical potential from a common starting point in terms of skill and technique.

Have students collect their own instruments. Emphasize the kinds of materials, sizes, and shapes that they can find and encourage them to find beaters of various types (sticks, nails, mallets, plastic rods, and so on) to use for playing the percussion types. The instruments will fall into one of the following categories:

- Metals: pans, pots, cans (both empty and filled), plates, rods, spikes, bolts, screens, refrigerator racks, old tools, silverware, and auto parts
- Glass: bottles, jugs, glasses and tumblers for rubbing on the rim with water, and jars (either empty or filled with water); these instruments need to be carefully handled and controlled to avoid breakage
- Ceramics: plates, cups, flower pots, and tiles
- Plastics: bottles, cups, plates, jar covers, food package containers, combs, pens, and straws
- Wood: boxes, rods, dowels, boards, and rulers
- Paper and cardboard; bags, newspaper, cellophane, tissue paper, candy wrappers (for blowing), cartons, and tubes; paper can be torn, ripped, crumpled, rubbed, and scrubbed
- Rubber bands (stretched over resonating containers)
- The human body and voice.

Exploring Sound Possibilities

Let students explore ways they can play these instruments, and have them demonstrate different methods of performance. While the students experiment, set up a tape recorder. A recording is especially revealing and enjoyable for students: They can learn a great deal from hearing themselves play instruments and contribute as individuals to the group as a whole. Sound sensitivity and awareness can be greatly enhanced by this means. Now try some of the following warm-up projects with the whole class.

Call and response. Have one student be the leader by creating a rhythm or pitch-organized phrase on his or her instrument from the center of the group. (A circle is the best shape for class interaction.) Let the group respond by imitation, variation, contrast, augmentation, diminution, and so on.

Antiphonal. Have two to four groups go to different corners of the room and call and answer each other with patterned group phrases. Include elements of tempo, volume, and timbre (each group could have one type of material) in various sequences. Set up signals so that the groups know when to play.

Conversations. Let the students choose partners, and then have each pair converse with each other using an instrument as "voices."

Orchestra. Divide the class into groups of like instruments, and arrange them into a circular orchestra. Have a conductor stand in the middle of a the circle and, by turning slowing with outstretched arms, indicate which segment of the circle is to improvise. Arms raised high can mean loud; arms lowered can mean soft; and arms dropped to the sides can mean silent. Use two or more conductors and work out various signals between them. Note the gradual shifting of timbres that result from this exercise.

Number keyboard. Assign a number to each student and write the number on a chalkboard in the following fashion:

```
  1   2   3   4   5   6   7
  8   9  10  11  12  13  14
 15  16  17  18  19  20  21
             All
```

With the teacher as conductor (for the first time), point to various numbers on the "keyboard" and have the student corresponding to the number play his or her instrument. When the hand is removed from the number the sound should stop. A short line drawn under a number means the sound is to continue. The conductor then can go on to other numbers while others are playing continuously. Erase the lines when you want the sound to stop. "All" means "tutti"; use this sparingly. Various timbre patterns can be created by repeating number sequences. Textures can be built up with the use of the lines. Virtuosity can be the result of moving at faster rates from one number to the next. Choose a student conductor and repeat the work.

Once some of these large group experiments have been performed and recorded, the tape can be played back and a short discussion period can follow. These found instrument works now can be analyzed and evaluated in terms of pitch, timbre, tempo, duration, volume, meter, and rhythm. Such concepts of music design as phrase, texture, foreground and background, ABA form, and motive can be developed in these discussions according to the maturity and intellectual level of the group. Affective and imaginative responses also should be encouraged from the group: What were the emotional effects of some of the works? What kinds of moods and feelings were conveyed?

Small-Group Improvisations

Preparation. Divide the class into groups of five or six students, each group having heterogeneous types of instruments. Send each group into a separate corner of the room to plan an improvisation about three minutes in length. Depending on the types and ages of the students, the teacher may want to allow each group freedom to follow its own ideas or give them an initial structure (a story idea or a rhythm, contrast of volume, or bursts of loud staccato sounds contrasted to long, continuous, soft sounds). It is preferable, at this stage, however, to give as few instructions and to allow as much freedom as possible to draw out ideas from the students themselves. It might be helpful to have space in nearby rooms and hallways where the groups can be sound-separated. If there are any teaching assistants available, they can circulate among the groups to coach and advise. An alternative would be to appoint a leader for each group.

It is important during these initial small-group sessions that a free, relaxed, yet serious attitude be conveyed so that the groups will be encouraged to experiment and to overcome inhibitions and silliness. Each instrument in a given group should be given a chance to be heard. Overly assertive and zealous students need to be made aware of the needs of the group as a whole. The attitude that there are no "wrong notes" is also helpful. In these early sessions with found instruments, the groups will search for their own balance, design, and structure; it is important that they make their discoveries freely.

Sharing. After a fifteen- to twenty-minute preparation period, the teacher should call the groups together and get them ready to share their works with each other. The group to perform should be centered with the rest of the class seated in a circle or semicircle around them so as to achieve a modest stage effect and a performing atmosphere. (Do not overdo this.) Each work should have a title; have one of the students in the group announce the title as you begin to make the tape recording. Set up the microphones close to the performing group without distracting them or emphasizing the fact that you are recording; the live performance is the thing that is important. As the music progresses, the audience should listen attentively and quietly. Beforehand, mention the fact that a music performance is usually framed by silence.

Playback, evaluation, and discussion. The improvisations that result from these initial sessions with found instruments can be amazingly inventive. Often beautiful, free improvisations with delicate and fluctuating timbres result. A discussion and evaluation period should follow the sharing of all the groups. Topics should include student reactions, whether the work came out in performance as it had been planned, how each group decided what to do, the most exciting element in a work, combinations of sounds, and interesting rhythm patterns. The discussion also can include music terms and concepts according to the level and curiosity of the class.

Expanding Attitudes Toward Sound

The effectiveness of found instrument sessions often depends on the students' attitudes toward the kinds of sounds that are produced by seemingly primitive and potentially raucous instruments. A certain amount of aural preconditioning to the conventional music of our culture will have to be overcome so that students will be able to hear sounds freshly, acutely, and intensely.[1] The use of all sounds in a musical context is possible. The aesthetic significance of the sounds comes not only in their appropriate selection but in their arrangement in relation to each other.

One way for students to broaden their aural horizons is to have them attend concerts and listen to and discuss recordings of twentieth-century art music, jazz, electronic music, rock, and ethnic, folk, and classical music from non-Western cultures. We should try to understand the music of many cultures as well as of the different periods and styles of our own culture to increase our awareness of the total spectrum of musical sound. Only when a person becomes aware of the multiple possibilities of sound configuration and expression does he or she become musically enlightened.

Subsequent sessions of improvising with found instruments usually produce group works of increasing sophistication, control, and sensitivity. In the discussion periods that follow each session, students' self-evaluations will lead naturally to questions of how to improve to compositions. Any inhibitions on the part of some students will, by this time, be overcome by the enthusiasm that builds up through the self-discovery and participation inherent in the activities themselves. Now the students can continue their improvisation projects by using other sound sources and materials.

Further Projects

By expanding the concept of the found instrument to include the human body, a new and more personal spectrum of sound sources can be used. Groups of five to six students now can prepare their improvisations using tongue clicks; hissing; blowing and drawing air through the teeth, mouth, and nose; whistling; such nonvocal sounds as "puh," "tsss," "tuh," "kuh," and "sshhh"; hand-clapping with various timbres (cupping the hand in different ways); clapping on various parts of the body; knocking; rapping; and stamping. The concept of finding instruments in the environment leads naturally to the idea that all sounds can be considered music, a concept one might call "found music." John Cage differentiates between determinate and indeterminate music and argues that music is the absence of silence. What we deal with in improvising with found instruments is primarily determinate—that is, it is consciously controlled and arranged sound with an expanded spectrum of sound sources. The following suggestions for exercises using materials within that sound spectrum can lead to the realization of a true found music.

Sound walk (indeterminate music). Take the class on an environmental sound walk. Collect sounds from such sources as a school lunch room, library, gymnasium, boiler room, playground, street, supermarket, bank, place of worship, or city park. Make sound lists and classifications such as man-made sounds or natural sounds, roaring sounds, rustling sounds, twittering sounds, rhythmic sounds, low-pitched and high-pitched sounds, and so on.[2] Listen to and discuss the musical qualities of the sounds in terms of their pitch, rhythm, timbre, intensity, texture, heaviness, thinness, and so on. Write sound poems based on the sound walk. Use onomatopoeic words and graphic notation symbols, which can be performed musically. Tape recordings from a sound walk can be used to create works of musique concrète or can be combined with live sounds from found instruments.

Theater works. Improvise music to be played on the furniture in the room. Improvise music using only one method of playing, such as rubbing, scratching, dropping, rolling, rapping, or shuffling. Improvise music using only one pitch but many timbres or one rhythm played at various rates of speed. Improvise a work using everyday functions—walking, running, cooking, writing, washing, sawing, sharpening pencils—performed primarily for their sound value. Perform a work by opening and shutting doors and windows. Explore the spatial aspects of sounds: high, low, near, far, under, above, foreground, and background.

Sound and body movement. Combine found instruments with body motions. Correlate the sound with the appropriate motion. Reverse the process. Improvise music using mechanical motion with sound, flowing motion with sound, intermittent motion with sound, and so on. Create body sculptures and composite instruments (larger instruments that contain many smaller instruments).

Notations/scores/graphics. Improvise works with found instruments and notate them in originally devised notation systems. Use pictographs, diagrams, drawings, newspaper and magazine clippings, colored markers, paints, size and shape notations, fabrics, and so on. Then reverse the process by creating scores first and then realizing them in performance. Pay special attention to the visual effect and its relation to sound.

More found instruments. Improvise music using only one type of material such as glass, metals, or wood. Keep a "sound table" in the room. Have the students bring in new instruments each week. Construct a standing wooden rack from which to hang various instruments with fishing line. Collect Styrofoam packing scraps and picnic coolers that can be used to support metal rods, bars, spikes, and so on, without dampening their vibrations. Arrange them into "xylophones." Arrange a large collection of found instruments into an orchestra and compose works to combine vocal sounds, dance, slide projections, and conventional instruments.

Students can be encouraged to play with sound materials, combine sounds in various ways, and share their results with each other and with other classes. At the beginning levels there should be no wrong notes; all sounds are acceptable. Later, students can learn to improve their efforts according to their own development in skills, sensitivity, and imagination. A teacher can help them to set and develop standards in an open and relaxed classroom atmosphere. Creativity comes when students interact freely.

Improvising with found instruments can enhance students' understanding and appreciation of all periods and styles of music as well as of the basic terms and concepts of music structure. These activities also provide an approach to musical self-discovery and involve students in the creative process. Composing and performing with found materials and listening to and evaluating the resulting music provides a total aesthetic experience—an invaluable source of learning for today's music student.

Selected Readings

Articles

Ahlstrom, David. "The Sonic Event East and West." *Music Educators Journal*, November 1976, pp. 63-65.

Bristol, Marc. "Homegrown Music...and Musical Instruments." *Mother Earth News*, September/October 1978, pp. 126-27.

Carlé, Irmgard, and Martin, Isaiah. "Enlarge Your Sound Repertory." *Music Educators Journal*, December 1975, pp. 40-47.

Kaplan, Don. "How to Tickle a Whale and Other Everyday Activities." *Music Educators Journal*, October 1977, pp. 22-31.

——. "The Joys of Noise—Part I" and "The Joys of Noise—Part II." *Music Educators Journal*, February 1976, pp. 37-44, and March 1976, pp. 146-53.

Books

Cage, John. *Notations*. New York: Something Else Press, 1969. Facsimile reproductions of more than 300 scores illustrating a wide variety of visual configurations.

——. *Silence: Lectures and Writings*. Middletown, CT: Wesleyan University Press, 1976. Entertaining theoretical writings by the dean of American experimentalism.

Dennis, Brian. *Experimental Music in Schools*. London: Oxford University Press, 1971. A how-to book for classroom projects. Contains examples of graphic notations.

Dwyer, Terence. *Composing with Tape Recorders: Musique Concrète for Beginners*. London: Oxford University Press, 1971. Another how-to manual. Contains an excellent classification of sounds: tones, sones, mistones, and pseudotones.

Ernst, David. *Musique Concrete*. Boston: Crescendo Publishing Company, 1972. A concise pamphlet for classroom projects.

Montgomery, Chandler. *Art for the Teachers of Children: Foundations of Aesthetic Experience*. Columbus, Ohio: Charles E. Merrill Publishing Company, 1968. An excellent book for ideas in relating art projects to music.

Partch, Harry. *Genesis of a Music*. New York: Da Capo Press, 1975. A composer describes his own system of music organization and construction of instruments. Contains many fine photographs.

Paynter, John. *Hear and Now*. London: Universal Edition, 1972. Another manual for experimental classroom projects.

Paynter, John, and Aston, Peter. *Sound and Silence*. New York: Cambridge University Press, 1970. An earlier and more comprehensive version of the above title by Paynter. Integrates experimental music activities with those of a more traditional nature.

Russolo, Luigi. "The Art of Noises." In Apollinio, Umberto, ed., *Futurist Manifestos: The Documents of Twentieth Century Art Series*. New York: Viking Press, 1973. This article contains the "Classification of Noises" list quoted in many contemporary music texts. Excellent reading to discover the roots of "noise music."

Schafer, R. Murray. *Creative Music Education*. New York: Schirmer Books, 1976. Contains chapters titled "Ear Cleaning," "The New Soundscape," and "The Composer in the Classroom," all of which were published as separate pamphlets.

Selected Recordings

Environmental music

Animals of Africa: Sounds of the Jungle, Plain and Bush (Nonesuch 72056)

New York 19 (The Sound of the City) (Folkways 5558)

Sounds of the Humpback Whale (Capitol ST-620)

Musique concrète
  Beatles. "Revolution #9" on *The Beatles* (Capitol SWBO 101)
  Berio, Luciano. *Visage* (Candide 31027)
  Cage, John. *Fontana Mix–Feed* (Columbia MS-7139)
  Gentle Giant. *Three Friends* (Columbia PC 31649)
  Stockhausen, Karlheinz. *Gesange der Junglinge* (Deutsche Grammophon DG 138811)
  Yes. *Tales from Topographic Oceans* (Atlantic 908)

Percussion and piano
  Antheil, George. *Ballet méchanique* (Telefunken 642196)

Cage, John. *Music for Keyboard 1935-48* (Columbia CM2S-819)
Crumb, George. *Macrokosmos III: Music for a Summer Evening* (Nonesuch 71311)
Stockhausen, Karlheinz. *Zyklu1* (Mainstream 5003)
Varèse, Edgard. *Ionization* (Columbia MS-6146)

New timbres
  Partch, Harry. *The Music of Harry Partch* (Columbia MS-7207)
  Sounds of New Music (Folkways FX 6160)

1610-02-1.5M-12/91